From Timid to Tiger

A Treatment Manual for Parenting the Anxi

Dr Sam Cartwright-Hatton
with
Dr Ben Laskey
Dr Stewart Rust
Dr Deborah McNally

WILEY-BLACKWELL

A John Wiley & Sons, Ltd., Publication

This edition first published 2010
© 2010 John Wiley & Sons Ltd.

Wiley-Blackwell is an imprint of John Wiley & Sons, formed by the merger of Wiley's global Scientific, Technical, and Medical business with Blackwell Publishing.

Registered Office
John Wiley & Sons Ltd, The Atrium, Southern Gate, Chichester, West Sussex, PO19 8SQ, UK

Editorial Offices
The Atrium, Southern Gate, Chichester, West Sussex, PO19 8SQ, UK
9600 Garsington Road, Oxford, OX4 2DQ, UK
350 Main Street, Malden, MA 02148-5020, USA

For details of our global editorial offices, for customer services, and for information about how to apply for permission to reuse the copyright material in this book please see our website at www.wiley.com/wiley-blackwell.

The right of Sam Cartwright-Hatton to be identified as the author of this work has been asserted in accordance with the UK Copyright, Designs and Patents Act 1988.

Library of Congress Cataloging-in-Publication Data

Cartwright-Hatton, Sam.
  From timid to tiger : parenting the anxious child : a treatment manual / Sam Cartwright-Hatton, with Ben Laskey, Stewart Rust, Deborah McNally.
      p. ; cm.
  Includes bibliographical references and index.
  ISBN 978-0-470-68310-1 (pbk.)
  1. Anxiety in children. 2. Cognitive therapy for children. 3. Parenting. I. Title.
  [DNLM: 1. Anxiety Disorders–therapy. 2. Child. 3. Cognitive Therapy–methods. WM 172 C329f
2010]
  RJ506.A58C37 2010
  618.92'8522–dc22
                          2010016192

A catalogue record for this book is available from the British Library.

Set in 10/13 Scala by Laserwords Private Limited, Chennai, India.

1 2010

From Timid to Tiger

This book is dedicated to ZB, who was with me (quite literally, in my tummy), the whole way.

Sam Cartwright-Hatton, Manchester, September 2009.

Contents

List of Contributors

Dr Sam Cartwright-Hatton
Clinical Psychologist and Senior Lecturer in Clinical Psychology
School of Psychological Sciences
Zochonis Building
Brunswick St
University of Manchester
Manchester
M13 9PL, UK

Sam Cartwright-Hatton is an academic clinical psychologist who carries out research in the development and treatment of anxiety disorders of childhood. She was the recipient of the 2009 May Davidson Award from the British Psychological Society in recognition of this work.

Dr Ben Laskey
Clinical Psychologist and Honorary Tutor in Clinical Psychology
Salford Child and Adolescent Mental Health Services
Pendleton Gateway Centre
1 Broadwalk
Salford, M6 5FX

Ben Laskey is a parent and clinical psychologist who lives and works in Salford. He co-ordinates and delivers parenting programmes for children under eight years in the city and works individually with children and families. He has a particular interest in child anxiety disorders and conducts research through the University of Manchester where he is an honorary tutor in Clinical Psychology. Ben is on the national committee for the BABCP and has spoken at national conferences on parenting and anxiety.

Dr Stewart Rust
Consultant Clinical Psychologist in Neuropsychology
Paediatric Psychosocial Department
Harrington Building
Royal Manchester Children's Hospital
Hathersage Road
Manchester M13 9WL

Stewart is a consultant clinical psychologist in Neuropsychology at the Royal Manchester Children's Hospital, where he works with children and young people with head injuries, epilepsy, brain tumours and metabolic conditions. He has previously worked in community parenting for seven years, delivering parenting groups to families struggling with children's behavioural difficulties.

Dr Deb McNally
Clinical Psychologist
Paediatric Psychosocial Department
Harrington Building
Royal Manchester Children's Hospital
Hathersage Road
Manchester M13 9WL

Deb is a clinical psychologist specialising in working with children and families in Salford. She has a particular interest in parenting and cognitive behavioural interventions.

Preface

Amelia has just got home from school. She is in floods of tears. Her teacher gave the class a new red pencil each, and told them there would be 'big trouble' for anyone who lost it. Amelia has lost her pencil. She is terrified of what will happen when her teacher finds out.

This happens a lot. Amelia is often to be found in tears over some minor catastrophe, and is increasingly difficult to console. After several hours of failing to stem the tears, her Dad gets in the car, and trawls the corner stores and petrol stations. His luck is in, and he returns just in time for bed, with a shiny, new, red pencil.

Problem solved. Or is it?

Did Amelia's Dad do the right thing? Although he did the kind thing, did he do the best thing for helping Amelia cope with her anxieties in the long term?

Parents of anxious children are frequently faced with dilemmas like these. And, unfortunately, the average parent's instinct to protect their vulnerable child may be working in quite the opposite direction to that which is needed.

Many parents who come to see us already recognise that their approach is not working. They want help with getting it right. Unfortunately, in most developed societies, parents are left alone to work out how to bring up their children. This is difficult when you have a well-adjusted child. When your child is doing things that are out of the ordinary, it can be quite impossible.

This course is designed for parents like Amelia's. It is grounded in theory and based on empirical data. The course takes the therapist and parent through a step-by-step approach to managing anxiety in young children. It is aimed at producing confident parents who know how to encourage confidence in their child, who know what to do when their child is worried or afraid.

We have found this course very useful in helping countless families like Amelia's. We have also had a lot of fun along the way. We hope that you do too.

Who Is This Book For?

This book is aimed primarily at mental health professionals. Although we think that a wide range of people who work with children and families will find the ideas useful, we think that to run the complete programme, a core professional background in mental health is needed.

In addition, to get the most out of the programme, at least one group leader needs some training and experience in cognitive behaviour therapy (CBT) and one in behavioural parent training. Ideally, between them, the group leaders would be highly skilled in both of these.

In terms of CBT knowledge, at least one of the group leaders needs to be skilled in basic CBT techniques, including simple formulation, socratic questioning, behavioural experiments, graded exposure and cognitive challenging. He/she should also understand the basic CBT model of anxiety, including the role of anxious thoughts, the fight/flight response and avoidance.

In terms of parent training, at least one of the group leaders needs to be highly experienced in working with parents. He/she also needs to be familiar with at least one behaviourally based parent training programme, such as Webster-Stratton's Incredible Years, Triple P and so on. He/she should have a good basic understanding of behavioural theory, particularly the role of reinforcement and extinction schedules, and of attachment theory and of social learning theory. Outcomes will be much better if at least one group leader has led previous behavioural parent training groups.

Acknowledgements

We are indebted to a number of people who have supported us in developing this programme for anxious children. Dr Caroline White developed the renowned parenting service in Manchester and has been generous in sharing her creative, compassionate solutions to working with parents. Many of the ideas in this book are credited to her. Many others, whose source is lost in the mists of time, will doubtless have begun with her.

Sam Cartwright-Hatton would like to acknowledge a deep well of gratitude and affection to the late Prof. Richard Harrington, whose faith in this little idea and in her ability to develop and trial it, made this book possible. You are still much missed Dick.

The authors and publisher are grateful for permission to reuse material from *Coping with an Anxious or Depressed Child*, Sam Cartwright-Hatton, ©(2007) (Oneworld Publications).

The authors and publisher gratefully acknowledge the permission granted to reproduce the copyright material in this book.

Every effort has been made to trace copyright holders and to obtain their permission for the use of copyright material. The publisher apologises for any errors or omissions in the above list and would be grateful if notified of any corrections that should be incorporated in future reprints or editions of this book.

CHAPTER ONE

Theoretical Background to the Programme

This programme draws elements from two broad classes of intervention that have been shown, over many decades, to be useful for other groups of clients. The first is cognitive behaviour therapy (CBT) for anxiety. The second is behavioural parent training, a behavioural and social learning theory based intervention that has been widely shown to help parents of children with behaviour problems. The theory underlying these approaches will be briefly outlined, and we will explain how we use them in this programme to help children to overcome their anxiety.

▶ Cognitive Behaviour Therapy (CBT)

A very brief history of CBT

CBT has been practiced in its current form since the 1950s when psychiatrists and psychologists, such as Dr Aaron T Beck and Dr Aaron Ellis, most of whom had been trained in the psychodynamic tradition, noticed that many of their depressed patients held a rather consistent set of unhappy beliefs. To cut a long story short, they discovered that challenging some of these beliefs led to increases in happiness, and CBT was born. Since then, increasingly sophisticated cognitive behavioural models of mental illness have grown, and have expanded to cover just about every category of mental health problem, including anxiety. In fact, it could be argued that anxiety disorders are the greatest success story of CBT. Conditions that were once considered untreatable by psychological means, such as panic disorder, are now treated routinely using CBT.

Does CBT work?

In Britain, CBT is now the treatment of choice for most anxiety disorders suffered by adults. The National Institute of Health and Clinical Excellence (NICE) (2004) recommends that CBT be used as the first line of psychological treatment for anxiety disorders in adults (there are currently no NICE guidelines for anxiety in children). These recommendations are based on the very large and robust database of trials, demonstrating that CBT is highly effective for anxiety.

It is only in the past 15 years that researchers have systematically evaluated the utility of CBT with children and adolescents. However, a recent review showed that CBT for mixed anxiety disorders was effective for about 60% of the young participants (Cartwright-Hatton *et al.*, 2004.) The research evidence base for this field is growing fast, and is almost entirely very positive. Indeed, the CAMS study compared CBT with selective serotonin reuptake

From Timid to Tiger: A Treatment Manual for Parenting the Anxious Child. By Dr Sam Cartwright-Hatton with Dr Ben Laskey, Dr Stewart Rust and Dr Deborah McNally
© 2010 John Wiley & Sons, Ltd.

inhibitors (SSRIs) for the treatment of anxiety in adolescents for the first time, and showed CBT to be about as useful as the SSRIs (Walkup *et al.*, 2008).

CBT has not been widely tested on younger children, but there is evidence to suggest that the cognitive model (see below) does hold true for them. However, it is quite difficult to do CBT with younger children, and as very few trials have included them, we do not really know whether using ordinary CBT is the right way to go. We will come back to this issue later.

A basic cognitive behavioural model of anxiety

It is a bit misleading to talk about 'the' cognitive model of anxiety, because there are so many different models. However, there is much overlap between the models. We have taken the main overlapping features of these models, and incorporated them into our intervention.

The fight/flight response

This is central to most of the cognitive models of anxiety disorders and explains that horrible physical sensation that you get when you are scared. We've all had it – dry mouth, palpitations, feeling sick, butterflies, sweating, tight chest, wobbly legs and more. When we get scared about something, our body releases adrenaline, to allow us to save ourselves from whatever is threatening us. This adrenaline gears us up to cope with the threat, by fighting it off, running away from it, or in rare circumstances, fainting. Adrenaline is powerful stuff. It works by increasing the supply of oxygen and glycogen-rich blood to our muscles so that we are ready to 'fight' or 'fly'. It increases our heart rate and blood pressure, and makes us breathe quicker. It takes blood away from our guts (they can wait!) and sends it surging into our muscles and our brain. As you can imagine, all of this activity makes us feel pretty funny. It can make us feel as if we are going to faint, have a heart attack or even go mad. However, the critical point here is that when we are in fight/flight response mode, we are extremely unlikely to do any of these things. Our blood pressure is far too high to faint (although as always, there's an exception here – see below[1]), and heart attacks during the fight/flight response are really very rare. Our brain is working overtime, and has a vested interest in being very clear-thinking, so there is really no time for going mad. However, according to the cognitive models, and myriad research that backs them up, these 'catastrophic misinterpretations' are a key component of anxiety disorders (Clark, 1986). When people think that they are going to go mad, or faint or die of a heart attack, they naturally want to take evasive action. They will do whatever they can to get out of the situation that is making them feel this way. Indeed, the feelings and catastrophic misinterpretations can be so horrible that people avoid ever going into the trigger situation again, and this is when the anxiety disorder really starts ....

Avoidance

Avoiding things that make us feel bad is another key feature of all anxiety disorders. We can think of no cognitive model of anxiety that does not have avoidance at its core.

Avoiding things that make us feel scared, either because of the feelings we get in our body or because of what we think will happen to us (see Thoughts, Feelings and Behaviour below), causes problems for a number of reasons: First, if we consistently avoid a situation, we never learn that it's really ok. So, for instance, someone who is scared of spiders and will never go near one never learns that spiders (in the United Kingdom at least) really can't do you a bit of harm. However, someone who allows himself/herself to experience spiders soon learns that they are quite sweet, and can't hurt you, even if you let them crawl all over you. Spider phobics will often have built up a range of ideas about spiders. For instance, they will worry

[1] Some people can faint when they see blood or if they have an injection or blood test. However, if this has not yet happened to anyone's child, it is unlikely that they have this problem. For further information on this fairly uncommon condition, readers are referred to Ost, L.G. and Sterner, U. (1987) Applied tension: A specific behavioral method for treatment of blood phobia. *Behaviour Research and Therapy*, 25 (1), 25–9.

that a spider will get in their nose or ears (or other orifices!) and they won't be able to get it out or that they will choke on one. People who let spiders near them find out that spiders really have no interest in your crevices and are, therefore, perfectly safe. People who avoid spiders never find this out for real. They may 'know' it in their head, but knowing it for *real*, having experienced it, is very different. Second, if you avoid something that scares you, you never learn the skills for coping with it. You never learn how to calm yourself down or what to say to yourself. So, the fear carries on. Third, we know that avoidance grows over time. People who start out avoiding one thing, for example, spiders, soon start avoiding things that remind them of spiders, such as damp cellars, and then things that remind them of damp cellars, such as old houses. Over time, with avoidance, a relatively small fear can turn into quite a big one.

So, when it comes to anxiety disorders, avoidance is bad news. Tackling it is part of just about every model of CBT for anxiety, and this one is no exception. In the past, avoidance was often tackled by use of 'flooding'. Flooding involved making the fearful individual go face to face with their worst fear (e.g. stand in a roomful of enormous spiders). This technique was quite effective, as it tended to prove to sufferers, quite quickly, that they would come to no real harm. However, in the intervening decades, psychologists have become a little more humane, and 'exposure' to feared stimuli is done in a much more gradual, graded way. For instance, someone who is scared of spiders might now begin their exposure by looking at stick-drawings of spiders. When they feel happy with that, they might move on to looking at more realistic drawings of spiders, then perhaps photographs, then perhaps videos, before moving on to looking at real spiders in a tank and at a distance, before moving gradually closer, and eventually touching and holding spiders. This 'systematic desensitisation' is now the preferred way of treating most fears and phobias, and is the approach that we employ in 'Timid to Tiger'.

Thoughts, Feelings and Behaviour

So, if we have catastrophic thoughts, such as 'I'm going mad' or 'the spider will bite me', this can trigger physiological sensations that make us feel panicky and scared. Subsequent avoidance of the thing that makes us feel like this then leads to a full-blown anxiety problem.

This is the basic model of any anxiety disorder, and is the one that we present to parents in this programme. Our thoughts ('The spider will hurt me') lead to feelings (scared, panicky), which lead to behaviour (avoidance of the situation). This behaviour means that our thoughts never get challenged, and so the vicious cycle continues. We call this the Thoughts, Feelings, Behaviour (TFB) Cycle (Box 1.1), and we refer to it throughout the programme.

Box 1.1. The Thoughts, Feelings, Behaviour (TFB) Cycle

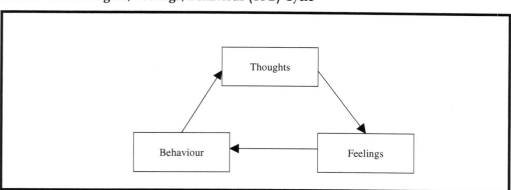

Psychologists now recognise that there is an almost limitless range of thoughts that can trigger this vicious cycle. For example, if someone is scared of dogs, they will often have catastrophic thoughts about dogs when they see one. So, for example, they might think 'It will bite me' or 'It is dirty and I will catch something off it'. Sometimes these *thoughts* on their own are enough to trigger a *feeling* of fear, and to cause subsequent avoidance *behaviour*.

Sometimes these thoughts will trigger others, such as, 'If it bites me, I might lose my leg' or 'I might get rabies and die'. Either way, if these thoughts are enough to trigger fear, and the fear is enough to trigger avoidance, then they are enough to trigger an anxiety disorder. So, for most anxiety problems, it is possible to construct a simple TFB cycle showing that *thoughts* lead to *feelings*, which lead to *behaviour*.

However, the TFB cycle is a very versatile beast, and as well as being useful for understanding anxiety, it is also very useful for understanding a wide range of other human behaviour. So, you will come across TFB being used for a number of purposes in this programme.

Metacognition

In recent years, psychologists have also realised that not only are thoughts important in anxiety but our thoughts *about* our thoughts are important too. So, for instance, we know that many people with obsessive-compulsive disorder (OCD) think that if they have a bad thought (for instance, about hurting someone) that this is as bad as actually hurting that person (e.g. Salkovskis, 1985). This is known as 'Thought Action Fusion' and is a type of metacognition.

Likewise, we know that people with disorders of worry (e.g. generalised anxiety disorder) will have all kinds of beliefs about their worry. Strange as it sounds, they often hold a set of quite conflicting positive and negative beliefs about their worry at the same time. So, people will often think 'my worrying will make me ill', but at the same time, will think 'I must worry to be a nice person' (e.g. Cartwright-Hatton and Wells, 1997).

These metacognitive beliefs are liable to make the person feel very worked up and anxious, and are likely to have an impact on behaviour. Positive beliefs about worries can make the individual engage in excessive worry. At the same time, fearful beliefs about the impact of those thoughts and worries will make the individual engage in avoidance type behaviour. This can be overt, such as turning off the TV when some worrying news comes on, or can be more covert, such as engaging in thought suppression or inappropriate distraction, both of which can make the situation worse.

Although this is a fairly new and complex area of CBT, we do touch on it in this course. In particular, when we have our session on managing children's worries, we talk to parents about the beliefs that they hold about worry, as we find that some of these can undermine their attempts to help their children manage their worries better.

The cognitive model and anxious children

The cognitive model that we have outlined above was initially designed for use with adults and older adolescents. However, research on whether the cognitive model holds for anxious children has, largely speaking, been very encouraging, suggesting that the same key components are present. So, we know that the thoughts that trigger the TFB cycle are likely to be similar for children as they are for adults, with some minor developmental differences. We know that children experience the same fight/flight response as adults when they are scared. We know that anxious children will try to avoid the things that they are scared of and that this will cause anxiety disorders in exactly the same way as it does for adults. So, the basic cognitive model of anxiety is the same for children.

However, using the cognitive model to treat anxious children is slightly different than when it is being used to treat adults. Furthermore, when the children are not being treated directly, but via their parents, this raises further issues that must be considered. In the next section, we will explain how we have managed these issues within a CBT framework.

How we use CBT

Thoughts, Feelings and Behaviour (TFB) and the Seven Confident Thoughts

One of the key aims of this programme is to make parents aware of how thoughts affect feelings and behaviour. We want them to understand this on behalf of themselves, and on behalf of their child. So, in the first session, we introduce the TFB cycle. This is introduced by means of examples of how adults think, feel and behave in stressful situations. We use some 'anxiety' examples, and also examples relating to general parenting situations, as we also want parents to be giving more consideration to how their thoughts and feelings affect their parenting. We return to the TFB model many times in every session. We spend very little time formally talking about how to changes one's thoughts; however, we do touch on this informally. For instance, if a parent acknowledges a troublesome TFB cycle, we will often say something like 'and how could you have thought differently about that?' However, we do no direct coaching on challenging the parents' own thought. Despite this, by the end of the course, most parents talk very naturally about their TFB, and many of them are able not only to spot troublesome thoughts, but to successfully challenge them too.

Having introduced the concept of TFB by getting parents to think about examples that are highly relevant to adults, we move on to thinking about children's thoughts.

We do not aim to produce parents who are skilled cognitive therapists by the end of this short course. That would be too long and complicated a process. Also, we think that parents have far more to offer than mere therapy skills. They shape their children's thoughts and feelings every day, in every single thing that they do. We think that parents can have far more impact on their children's emotions through the parenting that they provide than through any counselling skills that we could possibly give them. However, as will be discussed below, we do think that parents (as is the case for all humans) are more likely to make behavioural changes if they understand the reasons for doing so. This is where we introduce the Seven Confident Thoughts.

The Seven Confident Thoughts are a simplified system for understanding the way that an anxious child sees the world. They are distilled (by us, on the basis of no empirical data whatsoever) from the collective wisdom of many decades of cognitive research into anxiety and are shown in Box 1.2

Box 1.2. The Seven Confident Thoughts

The world is a pretty safe place
I can cope with most things
Bad things don't usually happen to me
Bad things don't pop up out of the blue
I have some control over the things that happen to me
People are pretty nice really
Other people respect me

We explain to parents that the goal of this course is to get their child thinking the Seven Confident Thoughts. Of course, it's not really that simple, but the Seven Confident Thoughts framework really gives parents something to aim at. Whenever we introduce a new technique, it is framed within the Seven Confident Thoughts, i.e. we get parents to think about which of the Seven Confident Thoughts the technique is working on. We have found that parents really like this framework. It gives them a clear, simple reason for using the techniques that we teach. Moreover, for some of the more psychologically minded parents, the Seven Confident Thoughts can help guide a whole range of other parenting decisions outside of our sessions.

The fight/flight response

We feel that it is critically important to give parents a thorough understanding of the fight/flight response. Many of the parents whom we have worked with have been very frightened by their child's physical response to fear. This isn't surprising really – it is worrying to see your child pale, clammy, shaking, crying, apparently struggling to breathe, and so on. It is even more frightening if you genuinely think that something awful is happening to your child. Very often, when a child is scared, the most appropriate parenting response is to sympathetically support the child in staying in the feared situation. Many of the parents we see actually sort of know this. Unfortunately, however, their instinct to protect their child from whatever dreadful fate is clearly about to befall them (a brain haemorrhage, a nervous breakdown?) trumps the more sensible messages that their brain might also be suggesting. Most of the parents that we have worked with in this programme have loved their children very much, and had strong desires to protect them from harm. In this situation, it is critical that parents understand the fight/flight response, and really believe that it cannot do harm to their children. So, we spend much of Session Three (Chapter Five) doing exercises that reinforce this point.

Reducing avoidance

As we have described above, avoiding fearful stimuli lies at the heart of most anxiety disorders. Therefore, anxious children need to do much less of this. Many families that we see are aware of this, but have really struggled to persuade their children to drop their avoidance, or, if they have persuaded them, have had very unpleasant experiences that have put them off trying again. So, we are presented with parents at varying stages of readiness for reducing their children's avoidance. Some need convincing that it is the right thing to do in the first place. Others are quite aware of this, but need to know that it can be done, safely, calmly and successfully, in a way that will not harm their children or their relationship with them.

So, we spend some considerable time in Session Three (Chapter Five) talking about the role of avoidance in anxiety disorders. We do this by means of a story – the Dinosaur and the Caveman, that illustrates the point well, and which can later be relayed from the parent to their child. We then use a standard cognitive therapy technique – a pros and cons analysis – to elicit parents' fears about reducing avoidance, and to address these.

Later in the programme (Session Four – Chapter Six), we begin to teach parents how to reduce their child's avoidance. In line with what is now seen as best practice, we discourage parents from using 'flooding' techniques, except where absolutely necessary. Instead, we teach parents to draw up fear hierarchies that can be used to provide their child with graded exposure to feared situations. We have sometimes found teaching parents to develop fear hierarchies rather difficult. Some parents grasp the concept very easily, and produce creative, sensible hierarchies at their first attempt. Others need much more help. Either way, parents will often run into problems (of varying degrees) when they begin to put the hierarchies into practice. For this reason, scrutiny of how hierarchies go forms a major part of the feedback in the first hour of all remaining sessions.

When working with anxious adults, it is useful to ask them to build little rewards into their exposure programme, and this is even more important with children. Many of the children whom we work with have very little intrinsic motivation to get over their fears, so their parents have to provide the motivation for them. This comes in the shape of little rewards, and lots and lots of praise. Using praise and reward to maximum effect are things that we teach early on in the programme (see below) and it is very important that they are tightly integrated into graded exposure.

Managing children's worry

Although we are not attempting to turn parents into expert cognitive therapists, managing children's worry is one area that does benefit from having a few basic therapeutic skills. After doing a bit of cognitive work with parents – in particular, discussing their metacognitive beliefs about worry, we go on to teach parents how to do basic problem solving and behavioural experiments with their children. When we were designing this programme, we had thought that this was a rather ambitious thing to try. After all, hadn't it taken us years of intensive study to learn how to do cognitive therapy properly? Well, as it turns out, the parents whom we see must be much cleverer than us, because they usually have no trouble at all picking up these techniques. Behavioural experiments are particularly popular, and having been taught how to use them, parents come back and regale us with all manner of creative and thoughtful behavioural experiments that they have done with their children.

Finally, we touch on the concept of 'worry time' which is adapted from the controlled worry periods that are used when treating adult worriers using cognitive therapy. This technique is used with adults to help them to increase their perception of control over their worries and to reduce the amount of ineffective time they spend worrying. Although we do not advise this for use with all children, we do present it to parents, and suggest that they try it with children who present with excessive worry.

► Behavioural Parent Training

Although Timid to Tiger is heavily informed by CBT, it is delivered with a modified behavioural parent training framework. In this section, we will give an overview of behavioural parent training, and talk about how we use it to help anxious children to become more confident.

Does it work?

Behavioural parent training programmes are widely used for the treatment of children with behavioural difficulties, such as oppositional defiant disorder and attention-deficit hyperactivity disorder (ADHD). They have been used for several decades, and evidence to suggest their efficacy for these disorders is overwhelming. Serketich and Dumas (1996) carried out a rigorous review of the behavioural parent training literature, and found 26 studies that met their criteria for robustness. These studies showed a mean intervention effect size of 0.86, which is very impressive. They also showed that results of treatment generalised to behaviour in school, and that parents who took part were significantly better adjusted at the end of the programme. Behan and Carr (2000) showed similar results in their review. There is also evidence that the effects of these programmes last in the long term. For instance, Webster-Stratton, Hollinsworth and Kolpacoff (1989) showed that improvements were sustained when they revisited families five years after they had received parent training.

Indeed, the Webster-Stratton 'Incredible Years' programme is one of the most well-established and well-researched behavioural parenting programmes for children with behaviour problems that is currently available. All of the authors of this book have received training in this intervention, and have found it invaluable. Further details on this programme and how to access their world-wide training programme are available in the Additional Resources section at the end of this book. We would strongly advise anyone interested in running behavioural parenting programmes to seek out this or similar training (e.g. in the excellent and well-researched 'Triple P' programme – see Additional Resources).

What it does and how it works

Standard behavioural parent training programmes are typically run with a small group of parents, who attend for a weekly session of around two hours, without their children. During sessions, parents learn new parenting skills which they then go home to practise with their children. The groups are normally run by two group leaders who have professional mental health backgrounds and are trained in the intervention. However, behavioural parent training can also be run with individual families. For further information on how the programmes run, see Chapter Two of this book.

The standard programmes (i.e. the ones developed for children with behavioural problems) are based on strong evidence that such children have parents who employ a number of behaviours that are thought to cause, or at least maintain, their child's difficulties. It is these parenting behaviours that the intervention seeks to modify. In the following pages, we will review the main components of behavioural parent training programmes, briefly explaining the theory on which they are based. We will then go on to show how we use these same components, to help parents of anxious children.

Play

Research has shown that parents of children with behaviour problems are less likely to show positive behaviours, such as praise and affection to those children (e.g. Patterson, Littman and Hinsey, 1964; Dumas, Lemay and Dauwalder, 2001). This is problematic for a number of reasons, as we shall see, but one difficulty is that eventually, it can lead to a rather cold and unfriendly relationship between the parent and the child. Clearly, this is not a good basis for a strong working relationship between the parent and the child, and the child feels that they have little incentive to behave appropriately for the parent. As we always say to parents, if you have a boss that you really like, and one that you don't like, and they ask you to do an extra bit of work as a favour to them, what will you do? Most parents agree that they would go out of their way to help the nice boss, but would be likely to dig their heels in and refuse to go the extra mile for the disliked one. Children are the same. If they feel warm towards the parent, they will be much more biddable.

Second, there is now a lot of research into 'attachment' and children's behavioural and emotional difficulties. Attachment theory was initially developed by Bowlby (e.g. see Bowlby, 1988 for an overview), who described the attachment of children to their caregivers as an instinctive developmental process. It is thought that this central relationship provides the key psychosocial experiences in children's development. Through their experiences of this central relationship, children develop an 'internal working model' of the world. Put simply, if this relationship is hostile and cold, then children will assume that the rest of the world is hostile and cold, and will act accordingly. On the other hand, if this relationship is warm and kind and supportive, then it tells the children that they can expect the rest of the world to be the same, and they will behave very differently.

In order to foster a strong attachment with the parent, and to put 'money in the bank' for later in the programme, where the parent starts to make demands of the child, the intervention begins by training parents in a form of relationship-building play. In this type of play (which is described in more detail in Chapter Four), the child is put in control, and the parent is there to give the child his/her undivided attention, and lots of warmth, praise, affection and encouragement. Done properly, this technique is excellent at rebuilding strained parent – child relationships, and we can each give countless examples of cases where children's well-being has improved markedly after the parents have attended this session.

Positive reinforcement of good behaviours

Research shows that in the vast majority of cases of behaviour problems, parents are under-using positive reinforcement strategies to encourage good behaviour in their children. That is, parents are using very little praise, and very few rewards to encourage their children to engage in good behaviours (e.g. Webster-Stratton, 1985). We know that children, like all other creatures that have ever been investigated, respond very predictably to consistent positive reinforcement. If a child receives fairly reliable, properly delivered praise for a behaviour (*any* behaviour) they will be more likely to show that behaviour again in the future. Children love praise – especially from their parents. They love rewards even more than praise, and will work really quite hard to get a small reward. However, the evidence suggests that parents of children with behaviour problems are unlikely to give rewards to encourage their children to work on good behaviours.

So, all good behavioural parent training programmes teach parents to give lots of positive attention, praise and small rewards to encourage their children's good behaviours. More details on how this is done are given in Chapters Six and Seven.

Setting limits and consequences

There is increasing evidence that parents of behaviour-disordered children are prone to not setting limits for their children particularly well. For instance, Forehand, Wells and Sturgis (1978) found that giving poor commands was predictive of non-compliance in young children. Moreover, other research shows that compliance rises once parents are taught to give commands properly (Roberts *et al.*, 1978). Clearly, if children are receiving commands that they do not understand, or cannot remember, they are unlikely to carry them out. So, all good behavioural parent training programmes include a component that teaches parents how to give commands in the most effective manner.

Research has also shown that parents of behaviour-disordered children are less likely to enforce commands than other parents. That is, if the child refuses to comply, the parent very quickly gives up trying to make them do so. This observation forms the core of Patterson's (1982) influential 'coercive cycle'. In this cycle, the parent gives a command, such as 'tidy away your toys'. The child refuses, perhaps using some aversive behaviour (e.g. crying, shouting), and the parent gives the command again, throwing in some aversive behaviour of their own, for example, shouting, or threatening to smack the child. Sometimes, the child will comply at this point, reinforcing the parent for their use of threats and shouting. However, most of the time, the child escalates the argument, perhaps by deploying a full-blown tantrum. The parent, often exhausted by repeated experiences of this nature, gives up, and leaves the toys untidied. The child has learnt that by displaying aggressive, coercive behaviours, they can avoid carrying out parental commands. It is well documented that if these coercive patterns of behaviour persist over time, they become internalised by the child and have long-term deleterious effects on their behaviour and emotional development. Moreover, the child takes these new-found techniques into the outside world, and uses them, to disastrous effect, with teachers, peers, and others (Dishion, Patterson and Kavanagh, 1992).

For this reason, all good behavioural parent training programmes spend some considerable time helping parents to overcome this coercive cycle. Parents are taught to only give clear commands that they know they can enforce, and to ensure that they do enforce them, using a range of considerably less coercive techniques.

Withdrawal of attention

Whilst parents of children with behaviour problems are *less* likely to give attention for children's positive behaviours than other parents, there is much evidence to suggest that they give *more* attention to undesirable behaviours (e.g. Patterson and Stouthamer-Loeber, 1984; Dumas and Wahler, 1985). As we have seen, when *any* behaviour gets attention from a parent, that behaviour will increase in frequency. This is particularly the case for children who do not get much attention from their parents.

This is because children are hardwired to get adult attention (particularly from their parents). We hate it when we get referral letters asking us to see a child because they are 'attention seeking'. All children are 'attention seeking'. They are meant to be. This is how they learn to be an adult – they do it by having interactions with adults. And, if the adults around them don't volunteer nice, positive interactions, then children will get those interactions, and that attention, in any way that they can, which can include using some very undesirable behaviours.

So, apart from helping parents to provide their child with lots of warm, positive interactions through play, praise and reward, all recent behavioural parenting programmes encourage parents to reduce the amount of attention that they give to children's unwanted behaviours. This also helps to reduce the coercive cycle that is discussed in the section above. In the past, some interventions did not include this component, and preferred to focus on just giving attention for positive behaviours, but research has shown that the intervention is much more effective if parents are also taught to withdraw their attention for unwanted behaviours. Details on how to do this with parents are given in Chapter Nine.

Punishment/consequences and time out

Perhaps as a consequence of their frustration at their child's difficult behaviour, we know that parents of behaviour-disordered children are more prone to using frequent, harsh and poorly delivered punishments for misdemeanours (Patterson and Stouthamer-Loeber, 1984). This brings with it a number of problems. First, it serves to give extra attention to children's unwanted behaviours, which we know is a bad thing. Second, it increases hostility between the parent and child, which is undesirable. Third, when poorly delivered, the child fails to learn new behaviour from the punishment. For example, we know that the effectiveness of disciplinary strategies for misbehaviours is influenced by variables such as timing (Abramowitz and O'Leary, 1990), length (Abramowitz, O'Leary and Futtersak, 1988) and consistency (Acker and O'Leary, 1988). Finally, the child learns that the way to manage other people's undesirable behaviour is to punish them, perhaps physically, which, in general, does not lead to good outcomes. In particular, much research has shown that the use of physical punishment is an ineffective means of improving self-control and compliance in children (e.g. Power and Chapieski, 1986).

So, most behavioural parent training programmes include a component, usually later on in the course, teaching parents how to manage those tricky behaviours that you just can't deal with by using more positive techniques (such as praise, reward, withdrawal of attention). Parents are taught how to use 'consequences'. These are mild, rapidly delivered punishments that 'fit the crime'. Parents are taught how to deliver these to encourage maximum learning on the part of their child (see Chapter Eleven for more details). Parents are also taught to use 'time out'. This involves putting the child in an un-stimulating environment for a short period of time only, and is a kind of super-withdrawal of attention. Time out has been shown to be very effective, in conjunction with the other techniques taught in the programme, for managing dangerous and destructive child behaviours (see Chapter Eleven for more details).

Social learning theory

Since the earliest days of child psychology, theorists have argued that children's behaviour is learned by imitation of their caregivers' behaviours (e.g. Bandura, 1977). In particular, children will copy other people's behaviour if that behaviour results in desirable outcomes for the person that they are copying. So, if parents frequently gets their needs met by shouting, hitting, or otherwise coercing other people, then a child is likely to copy that behaviour very readily. So, the whole range of techniques that parents learn (praise, play, reward, ignoring, time out, consequences) in parent training programmes are giving the child a much more positive model of how to get one's needs met. Furthermore, the group leaders are also modelling these processes to the parents in their group. Whilst running the group, group leaders use copious amounts of praise, attention and reward to encourage parents. They also use smaller amounts of withdrawal of attention, to manage situations where a parent is engaging in undesirable behaviour (e.g. dominating a discussion). So, the group leader models these techniques to parents, and the parents then model them to their child.

In this section, we have briefly covered the main theories that underpin behavioural parent training programmes. We will now turn our attention to how parenting processes might be involved in anxiety disorders, and show how we use the basic behavioural parent training techniques to modify these.

▶ Parenting and Anxiety

Parenting processes in child anxiety have received much less attention than those in behaviour problems. However, in recent years, we have begun to realise that parental processes are important for children presenting with internalising difficulties. For a detailed overview of this area, readers are recommended an excellent review by Wood *et al.* (2003).

Does it work?

Research into whether parenting interventions are useful in treating childhood anxiety is in its infancy. However, some authors (in particular, Belsky, 2005) are beginning to suggest that anxious children might actually be *more* vulnerable to parenting influences than their less anxious peers, and, therefore, benefit more strongly from parenting interventions. In defence of this theory, Belsky (2005) cites a number of lines of research. First, Kochanska (1995) reports that when examining maternal behaviour (in particular, the use of 'gentle' or 'negative' discipline), parenting was much more predictive of children's behaviour for children who were described as fearful or anxious, than for other children. Indeed, for the other children, maternal behaviour had very little impact on child outcomes. Unfortunately, this research was correlational. However, research with primates has shown similar effects in a more controlled experimental setting. Suomi (1997) reports research in which the impact of parenting on outcomes for rhesus macaques was examined. In this study, baby macaques were removed from their birth mother within a few days of birth, and fostered to either a macaque mother with average mothering skills or to highly skilled foster mother. The intriguing results indicated that for infants with an average temperament, the impact of the mothering received was pretty limited. However, for infants who were identified as highly fearful and anxious to begin with, the impact of the fostering was dramatic. Fearful infants who were fostered to average mothers did very poorly; they continued to display fearful behaviour, and showed highly reactive responses to minor upsets. Moreover, in adolescence and beyond, these macaques continued to perform poorly, ensuring that they were low in the social hierarchy and had limited access to resources. In contrast, the fearful infants who were fostered to the highly skilled mother macaques had very different outcomes; these infants became very confident. In the longer term, these macaques did very well socially, and rose to the top of their social hierarchies, ensuring privileged access to food and other resources. These studies give a tantalising indication that for children with an anxious/inhibited temperament, the quality of parenting may be particularly important, with those receiving poor parenting doing disproportionately badly, and those receiving good parenting doing disproportionately well. In other words, it is possible that anxious children are likely to be *particularly* sensitive to the effects of the parenting that they receive.

In light of the evidence that child anxiety is associated with some parenting impairments and that anxious children may be particularly vulnerable to the effects of poor parenting, Cartwright-Hatton *et al.* (2005) examined the effect of a standard behavioural parent training programme on the internalising symptoms of a group of young children. Although the 43 children were referred primarily with externalising difficulties, they also experienced substantial internalising difficulties. After receiving a standard behavioural parenting intervention, these internalising symptoms reduced significantly, and to the same degree as the reduction in externalising symptoms. The results of this study provide further evidence for the role of parental behaviour management skills in the maintenance of childhood anxiety. Furthermore, a randomised controlled trial of the intervention described in this book has recently demonstrated its efficacy in treating a larger sample of anxious children, in comparison to a control group who were not treated. At the end of treatment, two-thirds of the treated children were free of their main anxiety disorder, as compared to just 15% of the control group (Cartwright-Hatton *et al.*, submitted).

How we use behavioural parent training in this programme

This programme is based on a modified behavioural parent training programme. That is, we use the major components and delivery framework of a behavioural parent training programme. The CBT elements that are described above are fitted into this.

The main techniques that we use are as follows:

Play

As in programmes for children with behavioural problems, Timid to Tiger makes early use of a parent – child play technique. Once again, by the time parents are in contact with professionals, parent – child relationships are often strained, and it is important to get these onto a more positive footing right at the beginning. Second, as for children with behaviour problems, there is evidence that attachment may be impaired in many families of anxious children (e.g. Warren *et al.*, 1997; Muris *et al.*, 2000). In order for children to feel that the world is a safe place, it is vitally important that they feel that they have a safe 'base' and so it is important to improve the attachment rapidly. For these reasons, the second session (Chapter Four) of our intervention is devoted to teaching parents a special type of play that enhances the parent – child relationship. Parents are encouraged to practise this play with their children every day for 10 minutes or so, and we frequently see leaps in children's confidence from this session onwards.

Praise and rewards

Parents of anxious children have also been seen to be less adept at using praise and reward to get their children to engage in the behaviours that they would like to see. This is often for the full range of children's behaviours, but sometimes parents are just weak at using praise and reward to encourage the brave behaviours that their children need encouragement with. They often feel that their children should not need extra encouragement for behaviours that come naturally to their peers. Once consistent, well-delivered praise and reward are put in place, there are often dramatic improvements in children's willingness to drop their avoidance of feared situations.

Setting limits

Like parents of children with behaviour problems, parents of anxious children can be prone to not setting limits well for their child (e.g. Gallagher and Cartwright-Hatton, in prep), albeit often for slightly different reasons. We think that many sets of parents and their anxious children experience something akin to Patterson's coercive cycle that is discussed above. However, the coercion may operate in a slightly different way; In the case of anxious children, when the parents issue a command, the children, particularly if they are scared of doing what is asked, will begin to get upset. They will cry and beg to avoid the activity, and if the fight/flight response fires up, even start to look and feel quite ill. Sometimes parents (if particularly stressed) will become angry at this point, and will shout or threaten (much as in the original coercive cycle). If the child complies at this point, the parent is rewarded for the choice of coercive and frightening parenting strategy. In many cases, however, parents are distressed to see their children so upset, and will withdraw the command, teaching the children that they can avoid feared activities by displaying fear. In the long term, we think that repetitions of this cycle can contribute to the development of anxiety disorders in children, by allowing them to avoid feared activities, and by teaching them fearful behaviour displays that eventually become internalised. Therefore, an important part of our programme involves teaching parents to set carefully thought-out limits, clearly and firmly, and then sticking to them, even if the child becomes upset.

Withdrawal of attention

Much as parents of children with behaviour problems are prone to giving attention to unwanted behaviours, parents of anxious children are very prone to giving attention to fearful behaviours. As we know, giving attention to *any* behaviour will increase the likelihood of that behaviour being produced again in the future. For understandable reasons, many parents of anxious children give lots of attention to their child when they become distressed. Although it would clearly be inappropriate to ask parents to ignore all such fearful behaviour, we think that there are circumstances where the amount of attention that is given to these behaviours can safely be reduced. In combination with increasing the attention given to other (particularly more confident) behaviours, this has a powerful effect on changing the contingencies that children are operating under. There is also evidence to suggest that positively reinforcing anxiety symptoms in children, such as promoting or condoning avoidant behaviours, is characteristic of anxious parents (e.g. Barrett *et al.*, 1996). When parents have been given a clear understanding of the role of avoidance in anxiety, and the effect of attention on avoidant behaviour, parents can also be helped to reduce the amount of reinforcement that they give to avoidant behaviours.

Punishment/consequences and time out

There is evidence that parents of anxious children are more likely to use harsh and physical punishments than other parents (Krohne, 1990; LaFreniere and Dumas, 1992; Gallagher and Cartwright-Hatton, 2008; Robinson and Cartwright-Hatton, 2008; Laskey and Cartwright-Hatton, In press). Clearly, this style of punishment is frightening for any child, but it can be particularly damaging for a child who is already prone to anxiety. So, some time during this programme is devoted to teaching parents to use appropriate, mild, gentle, predictable consequences for unwanted behaviour to parents. They are also taught to use time out in Session Nine (Chapter Eleven), and a discussion of the impact of physical punishment also takes place.

Social learning theory

As we discussed above, children often directly learn their behaviours by watching valued adults around them. There is now strong evidence that this happens in abundance in anxious children. And, since the majority of anxious children have at least one anxious parent, there is often a lot of good anxious material for children to copy. For example, Muris *et al.* (1996) showed that mothers with high trait anxiety reported expressing fearfulness in front of their children more frequently than mothers with low trait anxiety, and that the level of maternal fear expression was predictive of the child's level of fearfulness. Similarly, Gerull and Rapee (2002) showed that when mothers pretended to be afraid of a toy animal, their young children rapidly displayed fear towards it too. There is now much experimental evidence to show that children learn to be afraid by watching or listening to parents, or by watching their parents cope badly with anxiety (e.g. Dadds *et al.*, 1996; Siqueland, Kendall and Steinberg, 1996; Whaley, Pinto and Sigman, 1999).

Therefore, the role of social learning is explained to parents, and they are helped to identify situations in which they might be prone to modelling anxiety or poor coping to their child. They are then given techniques to help avoid this transmission of fear when they spot it happening.

In the next chapter we will describe how to set up a Timid to Tiger group, and the general processes and principles that underpin it.

▶ References

Abramowitz, A.J. and O'Leary, S.G. (1990) Effectiveness of delayed punishment in an applied setting. *Behavior Therapy*, **21** (2), 231–39.

Abramowitz, A.J., O'Leary, S.G. and Futtersak, M.W. (1988) The relative impact of long and short reprimands on children's off-task behavior in the classroom. *Behavior Therapy*, **19** (2), 243–47.

Acker, M.M. and O'Leary, S.G. (1988) Effects of consistent and inconsistent feedback on inappropriate child behavior. *Behavior Therapy*, **19** (4), 619–24.

Bandura, A. (1977) *Social Learning Theory*, vol. 247, Prentice-Hall.

Barrett, P.M., Rapee, R.M., Dadds, M.M. and Ryan, S.M. (1996) Family enhancement of cognitive style in anxious and aggressive children. *Journal of Abnormal Child Psychology*, **24** (2), 187–203.

Behan, J. and Carr, A. (2000) Oppositional defiant disorder, in *What Works with Children and Adolescents?: A Critical Review of Psychological Interventions with Children* (ed. A.Carr), Routledge, pp. 364.

Belsky, J. (2005) Differential susceptibility to rearing influence: an evolutionary hypothesis and some evidence, in *Origins of the Social Mind: Evolutionary Psychology and Child Development* (eds B.J.Ellis and D.F. Bjorklund), Guilford Press, New York, pp. xv, 139–63.

Bowlby, J. (1988) *A Secure Base: Parent–child Attachment and Healthy Human Development*, Routledge, pp. 205.

Cartwright-Hatton, S., McNally, D., Field, A.P. *et al.* Randomised controlled trial of a new cognitive-behaviourally based parenting intervention for families of young anxious children, submitted.

Cartwright-Hatton, S., McNally, D., White, C. and Verduyn, C. (2005) Parenting skills training: an effective intervention for internalising symptoms in younger children? *Journal of Child and Adolescent Psychiatric Nursing*, **18** (2), 45–52.

Cartwright-Hatton, S., Roberts, C., Chitsabesan, P., Fothergill, C. and Harrington, R. (2004) Systematic review of the efficacy of cognitive behaviour therapies for childhood and adolescent anxiety disorders. *British Journal of Clinical Psychology*, **43**, 421–36.

Cartwright-Hatton, S. and Wells, A. (1997) Beliefs about worry and intrusions: the meta-cognitions questionnaire and its correlates. *Journal of Anxiety Disorders*, **11** (3), 279–96.

Clark, D.M. (1986) A cognitive approach to panic. *Behaviour Research and Therapy*, **24** (4), 461–70.

Dadds, M.R., Barrett, P.M., Rapee, R.M., Ryan, S. (1996) Family process and child anxiety and aggression: an observational analysis. *Journal of Abnormal Child Psychology*, **24** (6), 715–34.

Dishion, T.J., Patterson, G.R. and Kavanagh, K.A. (1992) An experimental test of the coercion model: linking theory, measurement, and intervention, McCord, Joan.

Dumas, J.E., Lemay, P. and Dauwalder, J.-P. (2001) Dynamic analyses of mother–child interactions in functional and dysfunctional dyads: a synergetic approach. *Journal of Abnormal Child Psychology*, **29** (4), 317–29.

Dumas, J.E. and Wahler, R.G. (1985) Indiscriminate mothering as a contextual factor in aggressive-oppositional child behavior: "damned if you do and damned if you don't". *Journal of Abnormal Child Psychology*, **13** (1), 1–17.

Forehand, R., Wells, K.C. and Sturgis, E.T. (1978) Predictors of child noncompliant behavior in the home. *Journal of Consulting and Clinical Psychology*, **46** (1), 179.

Gallagher, B. and Cartwright-Hatton, S. (2008) The relationship between parenting factors and trait anxiety: mediating role of cognitive errors and metacognition. *Journal of Anxiety Disorders*, **22** (4), 722–33.

Gallagher, S. and Cartwright-Hatton, S. Self-reported ineffective discipline strategies: a comparison of parents of anxious and control children, in prep.

Gerull, F.C. and Rapee, R.M. (2002) Mother knows best: effects of maternal modelling on the acquisition of fear and avoidance behaviour in toddlers. *Behaviour Research and Therapy*, **40**, 279–87.

Kochanska, G. (1995) Children's temperament, mothers' discipline, and security of attachment: multiple pathways to emerging internalization. *Child Development*, **66**, 597–615.

Krohne, H. (1990) Parental childrearing and anxiety development, in *Health Hazards in Adolescence: Prevention and Intervention in Childhood and Adolescence*, 1st edn, vol. 8 (eds K.Hurrelman and F. Loesel), Berlin FRG, Walter de Gruyter, pp. 115–30.

LaFreniere, P.J. and Dumas, J.E. (1992) A transactional analysis of early childhood anxiety and social withdrawal. *Development and Psychopathology*, **4** (3), 385–402.

Laskey, B. and Cartwright-Hatton, S. Parental discipline behaviours and beliefs: associations with parental and child anxiety. *Child: Care, Health and Development*, **35** (5), 717–27.

Muris, P., Meesters, C., Merckelbach, H. and Hülsenbeck, P. (2000) Worry in children is related to perceived parental rearing and attachment. *Behaviour Research and Therapy*, **38** (5), 487–97.

Muris, P., Steerneman, P., Merckelbach, H. and Meesters, C. (1996) The role of parental fearfulness and modeling in children's fear. *Behaviour Research and Therapy*, **34** (3), 265–68.

The National Institute for Clinical Excellence. (2004) Anxiety: management of anxiety (panic disorder, with or without agoraphobia, and generalised anxiety disorder) in adults in primary, secondary and community care. Retrieved from http://www.nice.org.uk/cg022 (2009)

Patterson, G.R. (1982) *Coercive Family Process: A Social Learning Approach*, vol. 3, Castalia, Eugene.

Patterson, G.R., Littman, R.A. and Hinsey, W.C. (1964) Parental effectiveness as reinforcers in the laboratory and its relation to child rearing practices and child adjustment in the classroom. *Journal of Personality*, **32** (2), 180–99.

Patterson, G.R. and Stouthamer-Loeber, M. (1984) The correlation of family management practices and delinquency. *Child Development*, **55** (4), 1299–307.

Power, T.G. and Chapieski, M.L. (1986) Childrearing and impulse control in toddlers: a naturalistic investigation. *Developmental Psychology*, **22** (2), 271–75.

Roberts, M.W., McMahon, R.J., Forehand, R. and Humphreys, L. (1978) The effect of parental instruction-giving on child compliance. *Behavior Therapy*, **9** (5), 793–98.

Robinson, R. and Cartwright-Hatton, S. (2008) Maternal disciplinary style with preschool children: associations with children's and mothers' trait anxiety. *Behavioural and Cognitive Psychotherapy*, **36** (1), 49–59.

Salkovskis, P.M. (1985) Obsessional-compulsive problems: a cognitive-behavioural analysis. *Behaviour Research and Therapy*, **23** (5), 571–83.

Serketich, W.J. and Dumas, J.E. (1996) The effectiveness of behavioral parent training to modify antisocial behavior in children: a meta-analysis. *Behavior Therapy*, **27** (2) 171–86.

Siqueland, L., Kendall, P.C. and Steinberg, L. (1996) Anxiety in children: perceived family environments and observed family interaction. *Journal of Clinical Child Psychology*, **25** (2), 225–37.

Suomi, S. (1997) Early determinants of behavior: evidence from primate studies. *British Medical Bulletin*, **53**, 170–84.

Walkup, J.T., Albano, A.M., Piacentini, J. *et al.* (2008) Cognitive behavioral therapy, sertraline, or a combination in childhood anxiety. *The New England Journal of Medicine*, **359** (26), 2753–66.

Warren, S.L., Huston, L., Egeland, B. and Sroufe, L.A. (1997) Child and adolescent anxiety disorders and early attachment. *Journal of the American Academy of Child and Adolescent Psychiatry*, **36** (5), 637–44.

Webster-Stratton, C. (1985) Mother perceptions and mother–child interactions: comparison of a clinic-referred and a nonclinic group. *Journal of Clinical Child Psychology*, **14** (4), 334–39.

Webster-Stratton, C., Hollinsworth, T. and Kolpacoff, M. (1989) The long term effectiveness and clinical significance of three cost-effective training programs for families with conduct-problem children. *Journal of Clinical Child Psychology*, **57** (4), 550–53.

Whaley, S.E., Pinto, A. and Sigman, M. (1999) Characterizing interactions between anxious mothers and their children. *Journal of Consulting and Clinical Psychology*, **67** (6), 826–36.

Wood, J., McLeod, B.D., Sigman, M., Hwang, W.-C. and Chu, B.C. (2003) Parenting and childhood anxiety: theory, empirical findings and future directions. *Journal of Child Psychology and Psychiatry and Allied Disciplines*, **44** (1), 134–51.

▶ Further Reading

Ost, L.-G., Fellenius, J. and Sterner, U. (1991) Applied tension, exposure in vivo, and tension-only in the treatment of blood phobia. *Behaviour Research and Therapy*, **29** (6), 561–74.

CHAPTER TWO

How to Use This Book

In this chapter, we will give an overview of how to make use of the book. We will detail the clients that it is likely to be most useful for, and what therapeutic skills will be needed. We will then explain how to use the material in the book, including what to expect of each session, how to organise your group, and what therapeutic style we have found to work best.

▶ Who Can *Timid to Tiger* Be Used with?

The programme was designed for parents of children with primary anxiety disorders. It has been evaluated in use with children with a range of primary anxiety disorders, including separation anxiety, social anxiety, generalised anxiety, panic, agoraphobia and specific phobias. We have not tested the programme with children who have a primary diagnosis of post-traumatic stress disorder, although a substantial number of the children that we have treated have been exposed to trauma, and have done well. Similarly, the programme has not been evaluated for children with a primary diagnosis of obsessive compulsive disorder, but we have treated a number of children who have exhibited symptoms of OCD, and they have also done well. In our evaluations of this programme, we have been deliberately relaxed about comorbid disorders. An awful lot of the children whose parents have gone through this programme have had difficulties other than anxiety, in particular, mild to moderate behaviour problems, and mild autistic spectrum disorders. These children also appear to have done well in the programme.

Since the programme is targeted at parents, rather than children, the parents need to fulfil a few basic criteria. First, they need to not mind coming along to a group. This is where skill in working with parents first comes in handy. If badly presented, inviting the parent of an anxious child to come to a group can sound as if the parent is being blamed for their child's difficulties. This needs to be avoided at all costs. Instead, we explain to parents that this is a course for parents who want to learn how to manage an anxious child or to increase their child's confidence. Most parents of anxious children have felt exasperated or 'at a loss' on more than one occasion, and, if it is well presented, they will jump at the chance of some advice. We will return to this later.

Second, if the course is to be run as a group, which is what we usually do, the parent needs to have sufficient knowledge of English to stay afloat. If their English is weak, it may be better to offer individual support.

Finally, if the parent has anything more than a mild learning disability, he/she may be better suited to individual support.

The programme is designed for children up to the age of nine years. It can be used with children as young as three years, and on occasions, when clearly indicated, it has been used

From Timid to Tiger: A Treatment Manual for Parenting the Anxious Child. By Dr Sam Cartwright-Hatton with Dr Ben Laskey, Dr Stewart Rust and Dr Deborah McNally
© 2010 John Wiley & Sons, Ltd.

with children as young as 30 months. With children older or younger than this, parts of the programme become less relevant, and other important factors would be missed, although many of the techniques that are described in this book could be used very effectively as part of their treatment plan.

The programme was initially designed for use with small groups of parents. Typically, groups will have between three and seven families. Any more than seven families, and it is difficult to give individual attention to everyone, and fewer than three begins to lose some of the benefits of a group, such as mutual support and sociability. However, we have, on occasion, run the programme with an individual family, and it works very well. Some of the techniques that are described in the book are clearly aimed at the group setting, but with a bit of imagination these can be easily modified for use with single families.

Finally, this intervention operates entirely through the parents. After assessment we do not see the children for treatment at all. As described in Chapter One, the results that we have seen from this programme appear to be as good as interventions (for older children) that treat the child directly. However, there is no reason at all why the children should not be seen in parallel for complimentary treatment (e.g. CBT) if they are judged suitable for this, and if resources allow.

How to Use This Book

This book is laid out so that each chapter (after this one) describes a single session of the programme. The full programme lasts for 10 sessions, each of two hours.

Using the Material

Ordering

The material in the book is laid out in a very specific order. Those readers who are familiar with other parent training programmes will note that we have followed the time honoured tradition of including material aimed at increasing parent – child attachment and at increasing positive behaviours, before we turn to techniques for extinguishing less desirable ones. There is now a substantial evidence base supporting this ordering of material, and although it can be frustrating for parents (who want to know how to stop Little Johnny doing x, y and z), we would urge you not to alter the order. As you will see when reading through the session chapters, we provide lots of ways of explaining this ordering to parents, and of convincing them to bear with us.

Scripts

Throughout the book, we have provided scripts for many of the techniques that we use. But don't worry, we really don't expect you to learn these by heart. Instead, they are there to give a life-like illustration of what the technique 'looks like' and to give an indication of our delivery style. Rather than learning the scripts, we expect that most group leaders will take the general gist of the technique, note the main messages that need to be transmitted to parents, and then improvise their own unique script. Apart from anything else, all group leaders have their own unique style, and it would feel very strange just parroting someone else's words. Moreover, we urge you to make this programme your own – embellish our scripts, make them sillier or invent some of your own.

Using a cognitive behavioural delivery style

In cognitive behaviour therapy (CBT), the client is encouraged to become the expert on his/her own mind. Likewise, in this programme, the parents are encouraged to be the expert on their own child. Rather than simply equip the parent with a series of techniques, we want them to leave with a deeper understanding of their child, their child's difficulties, and themselves as parents. In this way, when new difficulties arise (as they always will) they will be able to confidently formulate a solution without recourse to an outside 'expert'. So, we aim to provide parents with a clear basic model of what causes and maintains anxiety in children. We encourage them to understand how processes, both internal and external to the children, can influence their state of mind, and how they, as parents, can help in this process. We achieve this by a number of means, many of which are drawn from the principles of CBT.

Formulation

In regular, individual CBT, the personalised cognitive behavioural formulation is central to successful treatment. Obviously, when following a manualised treatment, there is no room for a totally idiosyncratic approach. However, we find that forming and constantly updating (if only in our heads) a simple formulation for each parent–child dyad really helps us to give each parent the best service that we can. This formulation cannot, of course, be as detailed as it would be if treating an individual – apart from anything else, it would be impossible to remember so many complex formulations all at the same time. Nonetheless, it is possible to remember key points about each parent–child and weave these into the intervention. Usually, after the end of each session, we have a chat about how it went, and review how each family is getting along. If a useful new piece of information about a family has come to light, we will make a note of this, and think about how we will act on this in subsequent sessions. For instance, it often becomes apparent, sooner or later, that certain parents in the group are themselves very anxious, and that this is impacting on their parenting. In one case, it became clear that a very anxious mother was getting very distressed about her child's health. The child did have some physical health concerns, but these were not very serious. However, this mother panicked whenever the child displayed any symptoms, and it seemed likely that this distress was being modelled by the child whose symptoms were then exacerbated. We were able to talk (in private, in this case) to this mother, and help her to use the material presented in the group to moderate her concerns, and to plan alternative ways of responding when she became anxious. In other situations, we have advised parents on sources of support for their own mental health difficulties, when these have become part of our formulation. And, on several occasions, we have given brief direct support to parents with mental health issues that were within our realm, for instance, brief management advice for dealing with a parental blood-injection phobia, which would not otherwise have been covered by the course. Finally, holding a brief formulation about individual parents and children allows targeted use of role plays and discussions. For instance, we knew that one parent became very distressed when her child, in a tantrum, said things like 'I don't love you'. We hypothesised that she would find this incredibly difficult to dismiss, and would, therefore, find the very important ignoring technique extremely difficult to deploy. So, when practising ignoring, we chose this parent as the model, and role played her child saying just this sort of thing. This allowed a discussion of how this sort of comment from a young child is very common and totally meaningless, and allowed her to rehearse ignoring it.

Socratic style

To achieve our goal of the parent as 'expert', rather than 'telling' parents what to do, we guide them to the answers, employing Socratic techniques that are used in CBT. Much has been written elsewhere on the use of Socratic techniques, and we do not have the scope to cover them in detail here. We expect that at least one leader of each group will be skilled in these techniques. Briefly, Socratic techniques, such as guided discovery, seek to lead the client to discover the answers to their difficulties, rather than being handed the answers by an expert therapist. So, rather than giving parents direct information, wherever possible, we guide them to using a series of well-targeted questions that are aimed at leading them to discovering the answer themselves. Many examples of Socratic technique are given throughout this book.

Principles

Another technique that we use, to encourage parents to take ownership of what they are learning, is 'principles'. We learnt this excellent idea from the Webster-Stratton 'Incredible Years' parenting programme. The idea is that when a parent says something that reflects an important concept for the programme, that parent takes ownership of that concept. The concept is written up on the flip chart, and the parent is invited to come up and sign it. So, for instance, if Bob says that he's been calmer this week, and has noticed that his children have been calmer too, that becomes a principle:

Bob's Principle

When I am calm, my children are calmer.

Signed ...*Bob*...

After the session, the principle is typed out onto a piece of card, and is decorated with fancy borders and clip art, etc. This is then laminated and stuck on the wall for every subsequent session. Then, whenever we need to reiterate the point that when parents are calm, their children are calm, we point to the principle, and say 'It's like Bob said, "when we are calm, our children are calmer"'.

Stories and analogies

When explaining difficult concepts to parents, we employ lots of analogies and stories, as is common in CBT. So, for example, in Session Three, when explaining the very important, but slightly complex, role of avoidance in anxiety, we use 'The Story of the Dragon in the Mountain'. Explaining a difficult concept in this way has a number of functions. First, it explains the concept in a much simpler and more engaging way than by just presenting the academic theory. Second, it is entertaining, and is almost guaranteed to grab parents' attention. Third, it provides a very 'transportable' means of the parent delivering the message to the child, should they wish to do this. Finally, it is very memorable.

We make use of lots of these silly stories and analogies in this programme, and we would encourage you to use them too. Telling a group of parents a fairy story can feel a bit silly the first time that you try it. But rest assured, they love it, especially if, as we do, you ham it up a bit. They understand that we don't think they are children, and seem to appreciate the amateur dramatics. Moreover, we think that stories work even better if they are ones that you have made up or embellished yourself. So, feel free to adapt our stories so that they fit with your personal style, or make up new ones to explain other concepts that we have missed.

Role plays and demonstrations

Role plays and demonstrations are used for very similar purposes as stories and analogies. First, they break the session up, and parents find them amusing especially if you are willing to make a bit of a fool of yourself. Second, they provide a much more memorable event than simply having something explained. Finally, they give parents a chance at a dry run and allow the group leader a chance to spot parents who are likely to have difficulties with the technique. When teaching new techniques, in particular, they allow parents to really see how the technique might work out in real life, and sometimes even a chance to practise it in the safety of the group. For instance, when we are teaching the 'ignoring' technique, we always do several role plays. These allow parents to see what they can expect (it can be pretty hairy the first time it is tried, and they need to be prepared for this) and allows them to practise their responses in session, so that they are not doing this for the first time when they are alone and overwhelmed by a child who throws tantrums.

When choosing a parent to help out with a demonstration, we always take a moment to pick the most appropriate person, and will sometimes even discuss this with our co-leader in advance. There are two key factors to take into account. First, it is important to pick someone who will cope with the exercise. Particularly early on in the course, it is a good idea to select a parent who seems fairly confident. Later on, more shy parents can be encouraged to take part, and will usually have developed the confidence to do this. However, it is important for all parents to know that they may always say 'no' to taking part. Second, it can sometimes be useful to pick a parent who is likely to struggle with the technique. So, returning to the 'ignoring' demonstrations, we like to pick the parent who we think is most likely to struggle with the technique. We then use our knowledge of that parent and his/her child to construct a role play that is going to push lots of their 'buttons'. This way, the group can support the parent in getting the ignoring right, and we can spot any areas that might need extra work. Most importantly, this parent has had a chance to practice this difficult technique in a supportive environment before he/she has to do it for real.

The final point to make here is that everyone hates the term 'role play'. If you ask for a volunteer to take part in a 'role play', you can be sure that everyone will look at their shoes. We find that this works better if you just call it a 'practice' or similar: 'OK, shall we have a go at that? Who wants to give me a hand? Sheila, do you fancy being a five-year-old for a couple of minutes?'

Key cognitions

Throughout the programme, we would encourage group leaders to be alert to parents' thoughts about the material that is being delivered. From many years of carrying out this and other behavioural parent training programmes, we have become aware of the importance of keeping an eye on what parents are thinking. We try to pre-empt major difficulties by using Socratic techniques in our presentation of material, but some techniques and concepts that we teach are prone to raising concerns in parents' minds. For instance, in our session using rewards to encourage more good and brave behaviours, we find that parents often have quite negative beliefs about giving out rewards for behaviours that they think their child should be showing as a matter of course. If parents hold this belief, they are unlikely to go away and try rewarding their child, or at least, are unlikely to attempt this with the gusto that we might like. So, whenever a new concept or technique is presented, it is important to make every effort to find out what parents think about it, and if necessary, challenge any misconceptions. In order to help this process along, we have listed a number of 'key cognitions' that you should try to identify in each session. These are the cognitions that, in our experience, are most likely to arise, and are most likely to cause problems for the parents. We also suggest ways of challenging these beliefs that we have found helpful.

Agony columns and handouts

There are handouts for every session. You may photocopy these to give out to group members. Some of the handouts have space for group members to write answers to in-session exercises, and these are clearly marked in the session chapters.

You will see that for most sessions, we have also included our Dr Esmeralda's agony columns. We originally just wrote one of these for fun, but it went down such a storm with our group that we wrote a whole set. Dr Esme's columns are designed to tackle some of the more common and troublesome beliefs that parents can hold about the material that we are delivering. For instance, in the session on rewards, she responds to a parent who thinks that rewarding good and brave behaviour will spoil her child.

Home practice

Home practice is an integral part of any cognitive behaviourally based intervention, and this programme is no exception. Each week, parents are given brief handouts to read, and are given some tasks to practice. Usually they are asked to focus on new skills learnt in the session, but also to continue rehearsing the skills that they learnt earlier on. It is hoped that the skills that they rehearse during home practice will eventually become habitual and be integrated into group members' everyday parenting practice.

We very rarely give out written exercises to do at home. We try to keep it as practical as possible. The exception is after Session Four, when parents are asked to devise a fear hierarchy for their children.

▶ Other Aspects of Delivery

Fun

We think that it's very important to make coming to the group fun. First, there is now an enormous body of evidence showing that learners of all ages assimilate material more effectively when it is delivered in an entertaining manner. Second, parents are giving up their precious time to come to the group – it will often be competing against multiple other demands. If it is boring or dry, there is no doubt that, on some occasions, those competing demands will win. Third, adopting a humorous style breaks down barriers between group leaders and parents. It puts people at their ease, and makes it easier for people to feel that they can speak without being judged, or without risk of being criticised. Finally, a number of quite difficult messages have to be delivered to parents in the course of this intervention. We find this much easier to do if it is embedded in the context of fun and humour. For instance, when we are talking to parents about the risk of modelling anxiety to their child, we illustrate this by using a couple of very silly and overacted vignettes. They make parents laugh, which enables us to start a friendly, open, and non-judgmental discussion of what children might learn from seeing their parents act in ways like this.

Non-critical

This is a related point, but clearly the intervention must be delivered in a non-critical manner. If parents are criticised or humiliated for their point of view, or for making a mistake, they are unlikely to offer to contribute again. They may even not return to the group. Therefore, we go out of our way to deal with parental mistakes or unhelpful beliefs in a gentle and positive way. We hope that this becomes clear as you read through the session chapters. In each chapter, we have given multiple examples of how mistakes and unhelpful beliefs can be gently challenged in ways that make the parent feel positive about themselves, their parenting and about making a contribution to the group.

Stickers

This often comes as a surprise to group members, but we like to give out lots of stickers in our course. We have boxes of stickers that are clearly intended for children's schoolwork, marked with slogans such as 'great work' and 'fantastic'. Beginning in the very first session, we give a sticker out every time a parent makes a useful point or some other contribution to the group. We do this in a very tongue-in-cheek fashion, so that parents do not feel that they are being treated like children. Although many are a little taken aback to begin with, a slightly ironic competition inevitably arises, with parents vying for the most stickers, and complaining noisily if they are not given one when they felt it was deserved. The reasons for giving out stickers are as follows: First, it adds to the feeling of relaxed fun that we aim to establish in the group. Second, it allows us to model *rewarding good and brave behaviour* in a very clear and simple way. Third, it means that parents have a plentiful supply of stickers to go home and use with their own children, so that they are practicing rewarding good behaviour.

Certificates

We always give out certificates for completion of the course. We show these off at the first session. Of course, some parents will not be motivated by our home-made efforts, but for some parents, the certificate that they receive at the end of the course is a real source of pride. We give the course an educational sounding title, rather than a clinical one, such as 'A 10-week course on childhood anxiety'.

The certificates are given out with much fanfare and applause at the last session.

Blaming parents

Whenever they are invited to come along to a 'parenting course', there is always the risk that parents will feel that they are being blamed for their child's difficulties. This is to be avoided at all cost. Apart from the upset that this causes the parents, it is likely, in many cases, to cause the parents to become defensive towards the course, and to devote their efforts towards defending rather than changing their parenting behaviour. So, we work very hard, during recruitment of parents to the programme, and during the programme itself, to ensure that parents do not feel that we are blaming them for their child's difficulties. You will notice, particularly in the first session, that a lot of effort is spent on this. It is also worth making efforts to ensure that parents do not feel blamed during the recruitment process. If they do, it is possible that they will not turn up to the first session. So, when we are 'selling' the programme to parents, we focus heavily on the educational component of the intervention. We sympathise with parents about how difficult it is to raise an anxious child, and allow them to talk freely about the difficulties that it presents them as parents and as a family. We then talk to them about how, in our experience, most parents do not actually want their child to be 'altered' or 'fixed' or 'theraped' but just want some good advice on the best approach to take when their child is frightened or worried. Most parents will readily admit that they feel torn between protecting their desperately anxious children and knowing that they have to push them to face their fears. So, having jointly established that the parents want some good advice so that they can manage the situation themselves, we introduce the idea of this course. We affirm that we only take 'good' parents on the course – those who care about their children and want to do the best by them. We reassure them that it is a small group of families who are in the same position, and that listening to others with the same difficulties is often a huge relief.

▶ Running a Group: The Practicalities

Room layout

We like to lay out the chairs in a horseshoe shape so that everyone gets a good view of what is going on in the middle. We put out a chair for each parent and each group leader – all together in the horseshoe.

At the front of the horseshoe is a flip chart and whiteboard. Most of the action then takes place in front of these.

There needs to be plenty of clearly visible space on the walls for sticking up posters, principles, ground rules, and so on.

Agenda

In line with a good CBT technique, we always write up an agenda before the start of each session. Ideally, this would be a collaboratively derived agenda, but as this is a manual-based intervention, that is not possible. Nonetheless, we write up the order of the session, including the feedback session, key new material and breaks.

Part 1 of the session – feedback

With the exception of Session One (see Chapter Three), each two-hour session is divided into two roughly equal parts, divided by a 10-minute tea break. The first part of the session is devoted to feedback from parents. In this part of the session, we go round the room asking parents how they got on with home practice this week. If we have a quiet group, we may need to ask someone directly how they got on. Otherwise we just open it to the group and see who starts things off. In beginning feedback, it is a good idea to open with a question that demands a positive answer, such as 'Has anyone got any nice stories about praise this week?' This ensures that the group session does not begin on a negative note, with a parent complaining about how something went badly. Of course, if something went badly, we need to know about this, but we find that it is best to start on a high note. Each chapter gives detailed information on the questions to ask in feedback, and how to troubleshoot problems that arise.

It is important to ensure that everyone gets their fair share of the feedback time. It is not uncommon for more confident members of the group to talk for long periods in feedback, meaning that quieter parents run the risk of getting just a few moments at the end. If this looks like happening, we politely bring the conversation with the more talkative parent to a close, by saying something like 'I'm mindful of time running away with us, so I'm going to move on to Sarah now, but if you're still concerned about this, come and have a quick chat in the break or at the end'. If someone consistently takes up a lot of feedback time, we might make sure that quieter group members get their go first by inviting them to speak earlier, and coming back to more talkative members later.

Part 2 of the session – new material

In the second half of the session, the new material is presented. This is outlined in detail in the session chapters.

Breaks and cakes

Each session is two hours long, which is far too long to expect anyone (parents or group leaders) to concentrate for. So, we *always* have a short break in the middle. Ideally this would be about 10 minutes long. In the break we have tea and coffee, and something to eat. We probably ought to be healthier, but cakes do always go down better than carrot sticks . . . . We think that it's important to use the break to pamper parents a bit. So, we always make the tea and coffee for parents, and try to have nice cakes or biscuits.

Ground rules

Coming to a group for the first time can be quite intimidating for parents. Even if they have been well briefed by the group leader in advance, they do not really know what to expect, and often arrive feeling very wary. Setting some early ground rules can go a long way in alleviating some of this anxiety. Setting of ground rules, about confidentiality, respecting opinions, and so on, is covered in the chapter (Chapter Three) on Session One.

Group leaders' roles

We have always run this group with at least two leaders. In our case, at least one of these has always been an experienced mental health professional with experience of both cognitive therapy for anxiety and behavioural parent training. We do think that it is very important that at least one of the two group leaders has this set of skills.

We also think that it is very difficult to run the group with just one leader. We have managed to run the odd session alone, in occasional emergencies, but it is exhausting and we don't feel that the group gets the best experience. Having two leaders present means that whilst one is focused on delivering the material/feedback, the other can keep an eye on process issues; for example, is a parent looking unhappy about something? Is someone not managing to be heard? Is somebody lost? The second group leader can also jump in and clarify bits that the first leader has forgotten, or has not delivered clearly. We do this a lot, and find that it makes the session feel very informal and relaxed.

Usually we arrange it so that one group leader takes charge of the feedback part of the session and the other takes the lead in part 2 – the new content. We rotate this weekly, so that the work gets shared evenly. However, if there is a good, open and equal relationship between the leaders (we would strongly advise this) then the edges do end up getting blurred a lot, and that is fine.

Key messages

You will notice that at the end of each session chapter we have given two or three 'key messages'. We recognise that each session chapter covers a lot of material, and it is very difficult to remember to cover it all perfectly – especially when you are running the course for the first time. So, we have written a few key messages for each chapter. Remember to cover these well, and you will not have gone far wrong.

Checklists

At the end of each session chapter, we have included a photocopiable session checklist. This is there for three reasons. First, it can be used to divide up the session and work out which group leader will present each bit. Although one group leader will take the lead on the new material, it is nicer for both if they both deliver part of it. Second, it can be copied and used as a quick guide to the session. Finally, we use it to tick off material when we have covered it, to reduce the likelihood of missing anything out.

Good Luck!

CHAPTER THREE

Session One

Introduction to the Programme and Some Basic Concepts

▶ Overview

In this session, group members are welcomed to the course. An outline of the 10 sessions is given, and ground rules are laid down. Some basic concepts are introduced, and some simple ideas for managing anxiety are given. However, the most important function of this session is to introduce group leaders and group members to each other, and to put everyone at ease.

▶ Before the Session

Arrange the room as described in Chapter Two.

▶ The Session

Welcome and introductions

We begin by welcoming participants to the group. We explain that the session will last for two hours, and that we will make sure that we will finish on time. There will be a short break in the middle for refreshments. We then show off the glamorous certificates that will be given out to those who complete the course. It is important to set the tone for the session very early on. We make it clear that although we will be dealing with some serious issues, it will be light-hearted, open, and fun.

Why have you come to the course?

This is a useful ice-breaking exercise, and is a quick way of allowing everyone coming to the course to see that they are not alone in struggling with their child's anxiety. Prior to coming to the course, parents often believe that they are facing problems that no one else has experienced. This exercise presents them with a clear challenge to this belief. In our experience, parents report this as being an extremely powerful benefit of the group. It appears to allow people to adopt a more hopeful approach to their children's anxious and

From Timid to Tiger: A Treatment Manual for Parenting the Anxious Child. By Dr Sam Cartwright-Hatton with Dr Ben Laskey, Dr Stewart Rust and Dr Deborah McNally
© 2010 John Wiley & Sons, Ltd.

difficult behaviour. We go round the group, asking parents to tell us about their children, say why they have come along, and what they hope to get out of the course.

Most of the parents will have heard at least some of what we talk about before, and it's essential to prepare them for this to pre-empt the risk of disengagement. We ask parents to bear with us when this happens, as we will often go into more detail than they've done before, and will let them in on some of the 'tricks of the trade'. For example, we've all been told to *'just ignore it!'* when a child is doing something that we don't like. But does it work? Many parents will agree that it doesn't. 'Well, this is because no one has ever told you how to do it. Ignoring sounds easy, but it isn't, and it won't work properly until someone tells you how to get it just right. That's what this course is all about.' During this discussion, it is important that group leaders demonstrate their confidence in the techniques the course will cover. We often say to parents that we *guarantee* that if they complete the course they will get all the techniques we discuss working more effectively than they ever have in the past. We might also use this opportunity to reflect on some of the positive feedback that parents from previous groups have provided. It is sensible to be realistic here; this won't mean that they will suddenly have a perfect child (as we know that they don't exist) but to emphasise that it will better equip them to cope when their child's anxiety and behaviour are challenging.

Also, some of the usual techniques that parents have heard about don't work so well with anxious children, unless you make some tweaks. Finally, of course, if they have had some useful experience of what we are teaching, they can share those with the group.

It is very important to reinforce several times in the early sessions that the course is *not* about blaming parents. We think that, in most cases, parents don't cause their child's anxiety, but we do think that they are in the best place to help their child grow in confidence.

Finally, we talk about how difficult it is being a parent. If you get a new washing machine, it comes with a manual, complete with a troubleshooting section at the back. With a child, you get nothing! Parenting is a really difficult job for which we usually get absolutely no training. Children are far more complicated than a washing machine, and yet no one ever tells us how to run them. In particular, no one tells you what to do if you get a child who is a bit out of the ordinary. Well, that's what this course is for. We will be your manual and your troubleshooting guide.

Ground rules

It is useful to set some group ground rules early in the first session so that everyone knows what is, and is not, acceptable. We ask the group to come up with these rules, but they may need a bit of prompting. Key rules to bring out are as follows:

- *Confidentiality between group members.*
  The same rule applies to us – the group leaders – unless we're worried about some harm coming to you or your children. If we are then we'll try to talk to you about it first and decide what we'll do about it together.
- *Arrive on time, finish on time.*
- *Turn mobile phones off, or onto silent.*
  If you have to take a call, leave the room.
- *Everyone is allowed to have their own opinions.*
  No one's opinions will be criticised or judged.
- *One person to speak at a time.*
- *Be respectful of one another.*

Groups may come up with additional rules as well and these will be included on the list as long as the group is happy with them (in one of our recent groups one of the rules was 'no jumping on the furniture'!). If there are any rules that are likely to cause difficulties in some way, the group leaders should facilitate discussion about potential benefits and drawbacks of the rule. In this way the group can reach its own decision on a final set of rules. It is essential that the parents feel a sense of ownership over the rules if they are to follow them.

We write all of these rules onto a large sheet of paper and stick it straight onto the wall. After the session, we type it up and laminate it, and then stick it on the wall for every subsequent session.

What are the behaviours that you find difficult?

At this point, we ask group members to list the behaviours in their children that they are struggling with, and these are written on the board/flip chart. Parents will usually list a fairly standard set of anxiety symptoms, including crying, clinging, worrying, refusing to sleep alone, shyness and so on. Once the list of anxiety symptoms has dried up, we ask parents to shout out any other behaviour that they find difficult. 'Does anyone have trouble with any other behaviour, such as aggression, refusing to do as told, etc?' We often find that this opens the floodgates, and, although parents have come with concerns primarily related to anxiety, they are struggling with a host of other behavioural difficulties.

This exercise fulfils two functions. First, it allows each member of the group to recognise that they are not alone in their difficulties. Second, it leads to a discussion of what drives these behaviours. However, in order for this discussion to work properly, it is important that each of the behaviours written on the board is a clearly operationalised *behaviour*. For instance, a parent may shout out '*scared*'. For our purposes, though, we need to know exactly what it *looks like* when the child is scared. So, ask the parent, 'what does your child do when he/she is scared?' and write down any behaviours that they list, such as 'cries'; 'throws things'; 'kicks out'; 'refuses to move'.

The second point of this exercise is to get parents to think about the effect that all of these behaviours have on parents. Ask 'What do parents do if they see any of these behaviours?' Parents will usually respond that they try to comfort the children, cajole them, reassure them, reason with them, shout at them and so on. These parental actions are all types of *attention*. Parental attention is very important in this programme, and we will return to it in every session. So, although we don't think that child anxiety is caused by giving it attention, we do think that parents can use their attention wisely, in order to reduce their child's anxiety.

The Attention Rule

What do children want more than anything else in the world? More than a new bike, a new Playstation (insert latest must-have toy), more than anything? The answer, of course, is attention. All children want attention – all children are attention seeking. They are designed this way. By making sure that they get lots and lots of adult attention, children ensure that they have lots of opportunity to learn how to be an adult, and to learn about the world. It is meant to be this way. We like to reassure parents that attention-seeking behaviour is normal and natural.

This constant need for attention is both a blessing and a curse for parents. Ask parents what happens if they give lots of attention to a behaviour. They will usually agree that they will get more of that behaviour in the future. This is because adult attention (particularly parental attention) acts as a powerful reinforcer of children's behaviour. We will come back to this point time and time again throughout the course of this programme. Finally, before leaving this section, it is important to reiterate that you do not think that parents have caused their child's anxiety, by paying it attention, but that, in some instances, we can use our attention to change the sorts of behaviour that children display.

Anxiety cake

One of the most important therapeutic goals of Session One is to reassure parents that we do not blame them for their child's difficulties. At the same time, however, we want them to leave the session feeling inspired that they can make things right for their child. This is a delicate balance to achieve. To do this, we start with the *anxiety cake* exercise, which is closely adapted from Dr Caroline White's wonderful 'Behaviour Cake' analogy. The point of the exercise is to demonstrate that although many different factors go into making up a child's personality, there are few that parents have any control over, and only one that they have total control over: *Parenting*!

Welcome to your food technology lesson! You get your money's worth here!

Write a simple cake recipe on the board.

Cake recipe:

4 oz flour
2 oz butter
4 oz sugar
2 eggs
Chocolate chips
Hazelnuts

What makes this cake taste good?

Someone will usually shout out 'chocolate' or 'sugar'. But what would happen if we didn't put flour in the cake – would it work? What about the eggs? Of course, with any of the key ingredients missing, the cake would be dreadful.

So, what is the moral of the tale? Children are a lot like cake – it's worth pausing here to let parents consider this. You will normally be rewarded by blank or questioning looks demanding more explanation. It takes a lot of different ingredients to make children the way they are. Ask parents to shout out the different factors that go into making children the way they are and write these factors up next to the cake recipe. Your list will be longer than the list of ingredients and in fact you could probably fill the rest of the session with this exercise if you chose to. We'd normally stop once we have 6–10 items on the list, depending on how talkative the group appears to be feeling.

4 oz flour	Temperament
2 oz butter	Genes
2 oz sugar	Learning difficulties
2 eggs	Parenting
Chocolate chips	Environment
Hazelnuts	Traumatic incidents

Make sure that you have got 'parents' or something similar on the list.

Just like the cake, what would happen if we changed one of the ingredients? That's right; it would be a very different child. You only need to change one thing to make a big difference. So, which of these things do we have the power to change? We can't change temperament or genes, or learning difficulties, or bad things that happened in the past. We can maybe change the environment a bit – school or granny, but we can't change the fact that we live in a high-crime neighbourhood very easily. However, there is one thing that we can change, and that is, how we parent.

Again, we don't think parents cause their children to be anxious, but we do think that they are in the best position to help their child grow in confidence. We think that parents who come along to this course are fantastic parents who are prepared to go out of their way to help their child through their difficulties.

Another analogy that may reinforce this message is the example of a car crash. If we feel it would help a particular group, we might discuss this after the *cake* recipe.

'We also think kids are like cars' (cue blank looks). 'Whose fault is it in this country if you're stopped at lights and someone drives into the back of your car?' (parents will say that it is the fault of the other driver). 'But, who has to call the insurance company, write letters, speak to the garage and get to work without a car for two weeks?' (us – the driver of the car that was run into). We emphasise that, 'As we can see from the cake recipe, many things outside parents' control have contributed to the issues that have brought parents to the group. However, it is parents who can make the most difference in children's lives and who have to put in the effort if children are to be able to make changes'.

Thoughts, Feelings and Behaviour (TFB)

The object of this exercise is to gently introduce a basic cognitive model linking emotions, actions and cognitions. That is, our thoughts, feelings, and behaviours are all related, and have a big impact on each other. Unfortunately, this deceptively simple concept can be quite difficult to get across. So, we have borrowed a couple of stories from Caroline White, to explain it to our group members.

TFB Story One – The motorway story

So, I want you to imagine that you are driving down the motorway, minding your own business, about 70 miles per hour. All of a sudden, another car swerves in front of you, nearly knocking you off the road. That car loses control and comes to a stop on the hard shoulder. You pull over behind.

What are you thinking about the driver of the other car right now?

Encourage the group to shout out what their *thoughts* would be. 'You bloody idiot, you just nearly killed me'. It is common, at this stage, for people to confuse *thoughts* with *feelings*, and so you will often get answers such as 'angry' or 'annoyed' or other unprintables. If this happens, gently encourage the group member to focus on what *thoughts* they would be having. Write these on the board.

Thoughts
That idiot just nearly killed me!

So, if that's what you are thinking, what sort of feeling or emotions do you think you'd be having?

Encourage the group members to shout out all the different emotions (or different words for similar emotions) that they would be having, for example, 'angry', 'annoyed', 'terrified', 'traumatised'. Put these on the diagram.

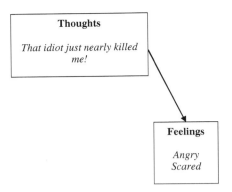

You may need to 'coach' parents to distinguish between emotions and thoughts at this stage. It is essential to emphasise the distinction at this point, as we will return to the Thoughts, Feelings, Behaviour Cycle repeatedly throughout the course.

So, if those are your thoughts and feelings, what would your behaviour be?

Encourage group members to shout out what their behaviour might be, for instance, 'go and bellow at the driver'; 'go and thump the driver' and so on. Write these on the diagram.

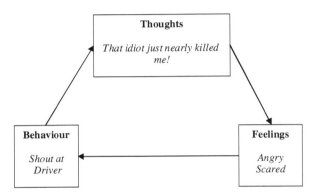

Right, now I want you to imagine that it's the next day, and once again, you are driving down the motorway, minding your own business. Would you believe it, it happens again, a car swerves in front of you, nearly knocking you off the road. It is out of control and ends up coming to a halt on the hard shoulder. But . . . this time as you look over into the car, you see that the driver is slumped over the steering wheel clutching his chest . . .

What are you thinking now?

Encourage group members to shout out what they would be thinking, for example, 'Oh, he's had a heart attack', or 'he's seriously ill'. Write these on the board. Again, ensure that you are extracting *thoughts* rather than *feelings* at this point.

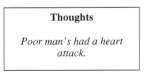

So, if that's what you're thinking, what are you going to be feeling? What will your emotion be?

You should find that people shout out very different emotions to last time, such as 'concern' or 'sympathy' although they may still find that they are also experiencing anxiety. Write this onto the diagram.

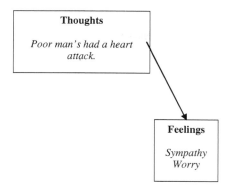

Finally, if you are feeling worried about the driver, and thinking that he must be very ill, what will your behaviour be?

You should find that most people want to go and help the driver, call an ambulance, and so on. Very few will want to go and shout at him this time . . . . Write this up on the diagram.

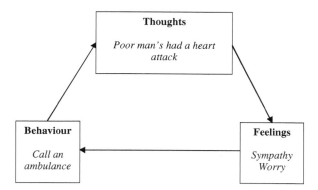

To enliven this example, you might role-play shouting at the driver. 'Would anyone want to get out of their car and shout 'What do you think you're doing, you idiot! Having a heart attack on the motorway! You nearly killed me!'

'So, two very similar situations, but two very different sets of emotions, and two very different sets of behaviours. What caused this difference?' You can subtly point at the 'thoughts' section of the diagrams here, if it helps . . . .

*That's right. The main difference was the way in which you were **thinking** about the situation. And we know, from many years of research into human thinking, that the way we think about a situation dramatically changes the way that we feel about it, and the way that we behave. In fact, if you go and train as a psychologist, much of the six years that it takes is banging on about just this – thoughts lead to feelings, lead to behaviour and this feeds back into your thoughts. We call this the **Thoughts, Feelings, Behaviour Cycle** or **TFB**, for short.*

TFB Story Two – The blackcurrant juice story

This is another story borrowed from Dr Caroline White, and nicely illustrates how our thoughts as a parent can influence the way we feel about our child, and the way that we parent our child.

So, let's have another story now, one that's about parents.

So, I want you to imagine: it's 7.30am, you've just got up. You get out of bed. It's freezing. Boiler's broken down again. You stagger downstairs, tripping over toys as you go. You get into the kitchen – water all over the floor

(How are you feeling? What are you thinking?). This is a bad day. Group leaders may choose to add detail or embellish this scenario. *'Never mind' you think to yourself, 'I'm just going to make myself a nice cup of tea, and go into my lovely new living room, which I've just had done up'. So, you go into your living room, with its lovely new cream carpet, and there's your toddler, sitting on the floor. He's delighted to see you, and leaps up to give you a kiss... and knocks over a giant glass of blackcurrant juice.... You watch as a livid purple stain seeps through your lovely new cream carpet....*

What are you thinking right now?

Encourage the group to share the thoughts that they might be having at that point. More open members of the group will admit that they are thinking some pretty negative thoughts about their child.... Congratulate them on their honesty, and ask if anyone else is thinking similar things – most people will be.

So, if you are thinking 'you little devil, you've just ruined my lovely new carpet', what feelings are you going to be having?

Encourage the group to recognise that these thoughts are likely to be leading to feelings of anger towards the child.

And if you are feeling really angry towards your child, what will your behaviour be?

That's right, you are going to be bellowing at the poor bewildered thing, maybe even a clip round the ear and sent to his room?

And half an hour later, when you've calmed down a bit, what will you think about what you did?

How will you be feeling?

That's right, you'll be feeling really guilty.

So what would you probably do?

That's right, you'll probably end up giving lots of cuddles, and plying your kid with chocolate biscuits.

So imagine this: you're three years old and you're watching the television. Suddenly your mum/dad comes in, starts ranting like a maniac, gives you a clip round the ear and sends you to your room, then half an hour later comes and gives you a cuddle and a packet of your favourite biscuits! How confusing is that?

So, this tells us that when we think negative thoughts, we get negative feelings, and that makes us behave in peculiar ways.

But don't worry if this happens to you. It happens to everyone, everyday. Humans are really prone to this. But, once you know about the TFB cycle, you can start to spot it, and you can try changing it.

This week, we want you to start looking out for your own TFB. See if you can spot it. We'll ask you if you managed to spot it when you come back next week.

The Seven Confident Thoughts

In this section, the Seven Confident Thoughts (7CTs) are introduced. The 7CTs are derived from the adult anxiety literature, and are a condensed version of the types of core beliefs that are thought to be critical in adult anxiety. This area has been much less explored in children, but as clinicians who work with lots of anxious children, we are confident that they are critical for children too. They are presented to parents for two key reasons. First, they allow parents a basic understanding of what is going on in their child's mind, and help parents to build a cognitive behavioural model of child anxiety. Second, the 7CTs become a framework upon which all of the techniques that we teach in this course are hung. You will notice, as we go through the course, that when a new technique is introduced, parents are asked to think about how this will help their child to develop the 7CTs.

Box 3.1. The Seven Confident Thoughts

The world is a pretty safe place
I can cope with most things
Bad things don't usually happen to me
Bad things don't pop up out of the blue
I have some control over the things that happen to me
People are pretty nice really
Other people respect me

From S. Cartwright-Hatton, *Coping with an Anxious or Depressed Child*. Reproduced by permission of Oneworld Publications.

So, we've talked a bit about how we think, and how that affects feelings in adults. Now we are going to move on to thinking about the thoughts that anxious and confident children have, and we think that these are very different.

Socratically elicit and discuss the Seven Confident Thoughts (see Box 3.1). We do this by saying something like:

We know that anxious children think 'The world is a dangerous place'. What does a confident kid need to think instead?

Yes, that's right; a confident kid really needs to think that 'the world is a fairly safe place'.

We then spend some time talking about why a child needs to believe that the world is a fairly safe place. This one is fairly obvious – if children think that the world is fraught with danger, they will not be able to stop themselves from feeling anxious. It is only when they believe that the world is safe that they will feel confident about setting out into it. While they think that it is dangerous, they will always try to avoid it, or only venture into it in the company of a safe person, such as their parents.

We know that anxious children think 'I can't cope with anything'. What does a confident kid need to think instead?

Yes, that's right; a confident kid really needs to think 'I can cope with most things'.

It is becoming clear from decades of research that confident people are those who have a feeling that they can cope with what life throws at them. People who feel that they cannot cope (even if they actually can) are prone to anxiety and other mental health problems. So, children really need to start developing the belief that they can cope with most things.

We know that anxious children think 'Lots of bad things happen to me'. What does a confident kid need to think instead?

Yes, that's right; a confident kid really needs to think 'Bad things don't usually happen to me'.

Again, the research shows that confident people don't expect unpleasant things to happen to them, whereas anxious people tend to expect the worst in situations. Expecting bad things to happen means that you are always on 'red alert'. It is hard to relax when you are feeling like this. Also, there is some evidence that if you expect bad things to happen, they are more likely to. So, it's important to get children thinking that bad things don't usually happen.

We know that anxious children think 'Bad things don't usually pop up out of the blue'. What does a confident kid need to think instead?

Yes, that's right; a confident kid really needs to think 'Bad things don't usually pop up out of the blue'.

Although we aim to have children thinking that bad things don't happen too often, it is a fact of life that we all have unpleasant experiences at times. However, we know that all people, including children, cope much better with nasty experiences if they get a bit of warning that they are about to happen. For instance, there is evidence that people cope better with bereavements if they get a little bit of warning that they are going to happen. This is because when we know in advance that we are going to have to face something difficult, it gives us a bit of time to prepare ourselves. Unfortunately, parents of anxious children have often ended up in situations where they don't give children advance warning that something unpleasant is going to happen – for instance, they will only tell their child that they have to go the dentist just as they are parking outside the surgery. This can mean that the child is constantly worried that something nasty is going to be sprung on them, and they stay in a state of red alert. It is easier to relax when you know that you usually get a bit of advance warning about difficult experiences and can tell yourself that 'bad things don't usually pop up out of the blue'.

We know that anxious children think 'I have no control over the things that happen to me'. What does a confident kid need to think instead?

Yes, that's right, a confident kid really needs to think 'I have some control over the things that happen to me'.

This can be a difficult one to explain to parents, so we use an example of good dental practice. These days, well-trained dentists are supposed to tell you that if you want a break when they are fiddling around in your mouth, you should just raise your hand and they will stop. Why is this? This is because having some *control* over what is happening to you is vital to feeling relaxed. Most people don't end up raising their hand very often, to stop what the dentist is doing, but just knowing that you can makes the whole experience feel so much nicer. The same principle extends to life in general. When we feel in control of what happens to us, we feel relaxed. When we feel out of control, we feel tense and nervous. Giving children control over their lives is very difficult – in fact, most children have very little control at all. Adults choose what they do and how they do it virtually 24 hours a day. So, instead, it is important that they begin to feel a sense of control over some small things. Many of the techniques that are taught in this course are about increasing children's sense of control over their world.

We know that anxious children think 'People are not very nice'. What does a confident kid need to think instead?

Yes, that's right; a confident kid really needs to think 'People are pretty nice really'.

How confident we feel about our lives depends, in large part, on how we expect other people to behave. If we have a picture of other people as hostile and unfriendly, new situations will always feel frightening. If people are generally not very nice, who will I turn to for help? How will people react if I make a mistake? Will I get into trouble? We all feel more confident if we have an expectation that people will respond well to us, be kind to us, and help us when needed. So, it is important to try to foster the belief that 'people are pretty nice really'.

We know that anxious children think 'Other people don't respect me'. What does a confident kid need to think instead?

Yes, that's right; a confident kid really needs to think 'Other people respect me'.

This is related to the last confident thought – i.e. 'people are pretty nice really', but is slightly different. People could be pretty nice, but still not have a lot of respect for me. There is now a lot of evidence that people who feel low in the 'pecking order' and feel looked down upon by others are prone to anxiety and depression. We all need to feel that we are worthy of respect, and that we can hold our heads high in public. So, it is important for every child to develop the belief 'other people respect me'.

Note that the 7CTs are not absolutes. The world is only a *fairly* safe place, and I only have *some* control over the things that happen to me, and so on. We do this because we want the 7CTs to be acceptable and believable. If parents think that we are trying to sell them fairy tales, then they will not be happy to teach the 7CTs to their children.

We often find that the parents in the group do not actually believe the 7CTs themselves. If this is the case, we have found that it's generally not worth getting into a big debate about this. Instead, we just ask parents to think about the impact of their child believing or not believing the 7CTs. For instance 'do you think that it's possible for a child to be happy and confident, if they think that the world is a dangerous place?' Most parents will agree that if a child believes the world is not a safe place, they have little chance of becoming a confident child. So, we are often left in the situation where the parent does not believe the 7CTs themselves, but are keen that their child does believe them. Of course, if some parents are struggling with severe anxiety difficulties, which often becomes apparent at this stage, it may be worth having a quiet chat with them about getting some support for themselves.

It is worth spending some time on the 7CTs, as these form the backbone of the course from now onwards. Make sure that you bring a large poster of the 7CTs to every subsequent session, and stick it up in a prominent spot.

Anxiety Pyramid

The order in which the elements of the programme are introduced is very important. We believe, as do many others who work in parent training, that it's really important to work on the parent–child relationship before you do anything else. We don't think that the programme can succeed without a warm relationship between the parent and the child. We then move on to using very positive strategies for managing children's behaviour, before finally moving on to the more aversive ones. However, reasons for this ordering are not always obvious to parents, and they can be frustrated that the course appears to be moving slowly, or is not addressing the issues that they think are most important first.

In order to address this issue, we have adapted the idea of the 'Parenting Pyramid' from the excellent Webster-Stratton 'Incredible Years Programme'. This programme is aimed at managing behaviour problems, rather than anxiety, so we have adapted the Parenting Pyramid to our needs, and rechristened it the 'Anxiety Pyramid'.

Print out a poster of the pyramid and show it to group members. Explain that we will start at the bottom, and work our way up to the top. Briefly describe each layer of the pyramid, without going into too much detail.

We then explain that many years of research into parents' courses shows that going up the pyramid in this way is the most effective way to do it.

Ask the group what would happen if you tried to build the pyramid upside down, with the top pointed bit at the bottom? Obviously, it would just fall over, and that is exactly what happens to the course if we did it upside down – it wouldn't work.

Reassure parents that although it can feel slow and frustrating at times, if they stick with us, they will get all of the information that they need to help their child grow in confidence.

Routines, diet, caffeine and exercise

Most of this session has focused on setting the scene, rather than giving useful direct advice that will have a rapid impact on children's anxiety. So, in order that parents have some practical tips to take home and start using, we provide some basic advice on routines, diet, caffeine and exercise.

Routines

We all know that we feel more stressed when things are chaotic, and this goes for kids too. In fact, it's even worse for kids who are anxious. So, to keep your child as calm as possible, it helps to have a bit of a routine that children can get used to.

Ask parents for examples of times in the day when they have family routines and how these tend to function. Encourage parents to reflect on how children respond to routines ('How do those bits of the day tend to go? What do your children do? How do they cope? Why?'). It may be worth asking people about parts of the day when there is less routine and going through a similar process of reflection about those times. Parents will usually report that their children are less stressed and anxious at times when there is a clear routine.

Ask parents which of the 7CTs this helps with. In particular, routines increase predictability for children and are therefore useful for helping children to feel that they have some *control* and feeling that *'bad things don't pop up out of the blue'*. Routines may also support other Seven Confident Thoughts targets.

However, having too rigid a routine can actually undermine children's confidence. Ask the group why this might be. The answer is that children need to learn to be a little bit adaptable. If they never learn to cope with little unexpected changes, then they are more likely to feel overwhelmed when they have to cope with big changes.

Diet

We all know the benefits of a healthy diet, and there is increasing evidence that feeding children a diet that is high in additives, fat and sugar is not good for their mental health (as well as their physical health). We don't spend a lot of time talking about this, as we are not trained dieticians, and we suspect that most parents already know what they *should* be doing.

However, there is one point that we do reinforce, and that is the need to have something in your tummy when you are doing something scary. We've all had that feeling when we are too hungry – you get shaky, and can't concentrate, everything just feels too much. Children are the same; so if they've got to do something brave, make sure that they have had something to eat, so that their anxiety isn't exacerbated by low blood sugar.

Caffeine

There is increasing evidence that children under the age of about nine shouldn't have any caffeine at all. Their little brains are very sensitive to caffeine and it could cause problems. However, the fact is that most children will have some caffeine in their diet, and parents should consider the impact of this on anxiety symptoms (or more precisely physical reactions that provide an excellent impersonation of anxiety). Parents of anxious children should be encouraged to consider limiting caffeine intake to avoid exacerbation of physical anxiety symptoms and, in particular, that timing of caffeine intake is quite carefully monitored. Many of us have had that feeling when we've had too much coffee – you get the shakes, and your heart races. You get exactly the same symptoms as when you are really stressed out! So, if a child has to do something scary, it is best to make sure that they are not high on caffeine at the same time – it will only make matters worse. Go through the list of food and drinks that have caffeine in them – there are lots of misconceptions out there. The following all have enough caffeine in them for a child to be affected by it:

- Cola drinks (yes, including diet cola). However, you can now get caffeine-free versions.
- Coffee, unless it's decaffeinated.
- Tea, unless it's decaffeinated.
- Green tea.
- Energy drinks.
- Plain chocolate.

Exercise

We all know that we should be getting lots of exercise, but few of us do. However, for some children, their exercise levels are so low that this could be contributing to their anxiety. If a child is cooped up in a crowded house, and never has the chance to go out and burn off energy (and stress chemicals), we think that this can contribute to anxiety problems.

Even if a child does do a bit of running around, there is evidence that doing even more can help with emotional health. Several studies have now shown that doing regular, fun, aerobic exercise, is as good at treating mild anxiety and depression as a few sessions of CBT. Although this research has been carried out on adults, there is every reason to think that regular, frequent exercise will have the same positive benefits on mental health for children.

Get parents to spend a minute or two thinking about what exercise their children do, and thinking of ways that they can gently increase this – for example, by kicking a ball around the garden for 20 minutes every evening, signing them up for a football club or swimming lessons.

Home practice

Watch out for TFB – try to spot your negative thoughts in stressful situations.

Key messages for the session

- Understanding how our thoughts interact with our feelings and our behaviour, including our behaviour towards our children.

- The Seven Confident Thoughts.
- Child anxiety is not the parents' fault. However, parents are in the best position to help their child grow in confidence.

▶ Key Cognitions to Elicit and Challenge

The main issues that are likely to arise in this session relate to the Seven Confident Thoughts. It is worth spending a significant period of time explaining these, and ensuring that parents are on board with them. As we explained above, trying to change parents' own beliefs, if they conflict with the 7CTs, can be time consuming and fruitless. Therefore, we focus on getting them to think about what they want their child to believe. For example, if a parent is struggling to accept that their child really needs to believe that the world is a safe place, then we would talk to them about how a child will behave if they think the world is dangerous. A child who believes this will not want to go out into the world will cling to carers and will worry about going to new places or doing new things. In other words, they will be anxious! We find that it is quite possible for a parent who believes that the world is a dangerous place to understand that they must try to make their child believe something different.

▶ Don't Forget . . .

- Although this is a manualised intervention, remember the unique individuals in your group. Try to think about how they will each respond to the material in this session.
- Keep drawing out 'principles' and referring back to those generated earlier by group members.
- Keep giving out those stickers to model reward and so that parents have a ready supply to use at home.
- Have fun! If you have fun, so will the group members.

Condensed session plan/treatment checklist

Item/concept	Group leader	Tick when completed
Welcome and introductions		
Why have you come to the course?		
Ground rules		
What are the behaviours that you find difficult?		
Anxiety cake		
Thoughts, Feelings and Behaviour		
The Seven Confident Thoughts		
The Anxiety Pyramid		
Routines, diet, caffeine and exercise		
Home practice		
Watch out for TFB		
Key messages to be covered		
Understanding how our thoughts interact with our feelings and our behaviour, including our behaviour towards our children		
The Seven Confident Thoughts		
Child anxiety is not the parents' fault. However, parents are in the best position to help their child grow in confidence		
Key cognitions to be elicited and challenged		
I don't believe the Seven Confident Thoughts		

Introduction

Basic things to help control your child's anxiety

<u>Caffeine</u>: Have a good look at how much caffeine your child takes in. Caffeine is usually found in tea, coffee, cola, and there is even some in chocolate. If you can't remove caffeine from your child's diet completely, try to keep it down to one or two times a day. It is a good idea to have a total ban on caffeine for the three hours before bedtime.

<u>Diet</u>: Have a look at your child's eating habits. We all know kids are allergic to healthy eating, but at least try to ensure that your child eats *something* every three hours or so. Anxious children can get worse if they are hungry.

<u>Routines</u>: Anxious kids respond well to routines. In particular, they benefit from eating and sleeping at roughly the same time each day. Obviously a busy family can't have a rigid routine, but try to keep things roughly the same. If you have to upset a routine dramatically, let your child know about this a few days in advance.

Looking into your child's head!

Childhood is the time when we are learning about the world around us. In fact, children learn things more quickly than any other age group. Children can learn something for life after just hearing it once or twice.

One thing that children are learning very quickly is all about themselves and the world.

The things that children learn about themselves and the world can really make a difference to their personality. We know that anxious children tend to be quite good at learning negative things, whereas more confident children tend to be better at learning positive things.

Things an anxious child might think about themselves

- *I can't cope with lots of things.*
- *Bad things happen to me.*
- *Bad things come out of the blue.*
- *I have no control over the things that happen to me.*

At this age, children are also learning a lot about the world. The things they learn can have an effect on their personality.

Things an anxious child might think about the world

- *The world is not a very safe place.*
- *People should not be trusted.*
- *Other people don't respect me, I'm bottom of the heap.*

It is usually no one's fault that children have picked up these ideas. Anxious kids just seem to pick these things up very easily. However, families are in the ideal position to try and change these ways of thinking. This course helps families find ways of bringing up their anxious child that changes their view of the world to a happier, more confident one.

The Seven Thoughts of Confident Children

The world is a pretty safe place.

I can cope with most things.

Bad things don't usually happen to me.

Bad things don't pop up out of the blue.

I have some control over the things that happen to me.

People are pretty nice really.

Other people respect me.

1

Things to Remember About Children's Behaviour

Children love attention above everything else and they will get it any way they can. Some kids even prefer negative attention (e.g. shouting at them) to none at all. Kids, and especially anxious kids, really love feeling safe and reassured, and will go to any lengths to get this.

Children often use language because of the effect that it has without understanding what it means. For example, some kids will swear, or say 'you don't love me', just to get attention.

The way that children think changes as they get older. They don't understand things the same as adults.

When children are upset or have to cope with change they behave as though they are younger; they regress.

Children don't understand time the same way as adults; they are tied to the here and now. For example, young children don't know the difference between next week and next month.

The way you interpret your child's behaviour will affect how you respond to them. For example, if you think they are having a tantrum on purpose to annoy you, you will feel angry and are more likely to deal with it harshly. However, if you think it is because they are scared, you are more likely to stay calm and deal with it differently.

Staying calm will help you feel more in control.

| TIME OUT |
| IGNORING |
| WORRY |
| LIMIT SETTING |
| EXPOSURE |
| PRAISE AND REWARD |
| ANXIETY |
| PLAY |

☺ **The world is a pretty safe place**

☺ **I can cope with most things**

☺ Bad things don't usually happen to me

☺ Bad things don't pop up out of the blue

☺ **I have some control over the things that happen to me**

☺ **People are pretty nice really**

☺ **Other people respect me**

Session Two

Securing the Parent–Child Bond through Play

▶ Overview

In this session, after feedback on home practice, we talk to parents about relationship-building play. This play technique really strengthens the parent–child bond and builds children's sense of confidence and security. It increases parental empathy towards the child and builds a foundation of trust on which the rest of the programme is based. Although this session does not focus directly on anxiety, it is a crucial one. The techniques and concepts that are learnt here underpin much of what is to come, and will be revisited repeatedly throughout the programme.

▶ Before the Session

- Arrange room as described in Chapter Two.
- Laminate 'principles' from Session One and stick them on the wall.
- Laminate 'ground rules' from Session One and stick them on the wall.
- Stick up a large 'Seven Confident Thoughts' poster in a prominent location.
- Stick up the 'Anxiety Pyramid' poster.
- Collect a bag of toys to be used in the session.

▶ The Session – Part 1

- **Welcome families**
- **Review the group ground rules that were agreed on in Session One**
- **Feedback on home practice**

Feedback will fill most of Part 1 of the session. It should follow the general guidance on feedback on home practice that is given in Chapter Two.

Content of feedback

Feedback should be focused mostly on issues raised in Session One.

From Timid to Tiger: A Treatment Manual for Parenting the Anxious Child. By Dr Sam Cartwright-Hatton with Dr Ben Laskey, Dr Stewart Rust and Dr Deborah McNally
© 2010 John Wiley & Sons, Ltd.

Thoughts, Feelings Behaviour cycle

Do parents remember this? Did they use it? Draw out as many examples from parents as possible. If there is any evidence of lack of understanding, go over the examples from Session One.

Key questions to ask:

- Who has noticed their Thoughts, Feelings and Behaviour (TFB)?
- Did you notice it with your children?
- Did anyone notice it anywhere else, for example, with your partner, or at work?
- How did your thoughts affect your feelings?
- How did your feelings affect your behaviour?
- Did anyone manage to change their feelings or behaviour?

Key principles to draw out:

- Using TFB helps me to keep calm.
- Using TFB helps my child to stay calm.

The Attention Rule

This was taught in Session One and is a key concept of the programme.

Key questions to ask:

- Who remembers The Attention Rule?
- Who has spotted behaviours from their children that were aimed at getting attention?
- How did you respond?
- Did anyone remember their TFB?

Key principles to draw out:

- It is normal for children to want parents' attention all of the time.

Responsibility and blame

We take every possible opportunity to reinforce the message that children's anxiety is not the parents' fault, but that parents are in the best position to help fix it.

Troubleshooting feedback

The most common difficulties that are raised in this feedback session are as follows.

- Parents have not done the homework (thinking about TFB). Gently try to find out why. If they just forgot, get them to try to remember whether there were any times when their thoughts affected their feelings and behaviour. Sometimes, parents just did not fully understand the concepts. If this is the case, go over the concepts again, giving more examples and ensuring that the parents have now understood. Remember, give parents credit for success but ensure that group leaders take responsibility for difficulties – for example, 'We didn't really make enough time to go over it properly last week . . .'.
- If any parents have not been able to think about TFB or The Attention Rule during the week, use Socratic questioning to help them to reflect on any child behaviours that they

might be able to think about using TFB for. Help them to think how they could adapt their own responses next time the behaviour occurs.

- Parents are sometimes still very worried about their children, and it can be easy for the feedback session to be diverted by this distress. Generally, if parents feel that their distress or concerns are not being heard and acknowledged, they will work even harder to ensure that group leaders understand how difficult and distressing their situation is. It is often helpful to reflect back on what parents are saying and to be empathic to the worries they express (reflect and summarise). However, there is a risk that this will result in loss of focus. This can be avoided by relating their distressing thought back to the TFB cycle and The Attention Rule. Use it as an opportunity to 're-teach' the concepts. Again, try to elicit alternative explanations and interpretations of children's anxious behaviour from the parent or other group members. In this way, you will keep the focus on discussing the content of last week's session. Reassure parents that as we progress through the course, they will start to get answers, but that we have to start at the bottom of the pyramid and work up. Emphasise that at this stage we would not be expecting things to have changed at home – we haven't even reached the first layer of the pyramid. Communicate confidence that things will improve as we work through the programme. In some instances, with parents who are regularly distressed, it may be worth planning a one-to-one conversation for 5 or 10 minutes before the session begins, to allow them to express their concerns in a way that impacts less on other group members.

▶ The Session – Part 2

Introducing Special Play

In this session, parents will learn a highly child-centred form of play. They will be asked to do this with their children for 10 minutes a day, every day. Introduce the following concepts Socratically, using examples and role play:

- *Play invests in the bottom of the Anxiety Pyramid.*
  Go over the concept of the pyramid. Explain that play is the foundation of the pyramid, and without it, the rest of the pyramid collapses.

- *Children learn through play.*
  They even learn when the play is non-directive and contains no teaching.

- *Play builds the parent–child relationship.*
  Ask parents 'who remembers playing with their parents?' Some will have happy memories of this, and will be keen to establish similar memories for their own children. A strong and trusting relationship is absolutely vital to the success of the rest of the programme.

- *Play develops children's speech and language.*
  In fact, speech and language therapists use a very similar technique to help children who are struggling with language development.

- *Play develops social skills.*

- *Rough and tumble play.*
  There is research showing that engaging in rough and tumble play with parents (particularly dads) is very good for building children's confidence and for helping them to manage aggressive feelings.

- *Play can be fun for parents.*
  Many parents really enjoy this special time with their children. Busy family lives and worrying about the child's difficulties mean that time for just enjoying your child is often forgotten. However, some parents report that playing with their children is difficult or boring. If this happens, discuss the difficulties in playing with children and compare these with the benefits. Normally, there will be short-term difficulties but long-term benefits.

- *Special Play is a happy time.*
  This Special Play is a way for parents and children to interact that is not focused around worries and fears.
- *Play builds the Seven Confident Thoughts.*

Teaching Special Play

In this type of play, which is similar to Sue Jenner's 'Child's game'[1], the parent's role is to watch and comment on the child's play. The child is meant to have *control* of the play. The parent should restrict his/her activity to describing, out loud, what the child is doing. However, the parent can get physically involved with the play if the child asks him/her to.

Here is a transcript of a dad doing this Special Play with his daughter Kiera. Kiera has chosen to play on the floor with a mixture of blocks and stuffed toys.

Dad: *Oooh, you are driving the red train along the road. You are very good at driving it.*

Kiera: *Choo Chooooooo.*

Dad: *Choo Chooooooooooo. Ahhh, I do like playing with you.* (Strokes Kiera's hair).

Dad: *Now you are making the dinosaur drive the train, ooh, he's going ever so fast. And you're going under the bridge. CRASH! The bridge has fallen down.*

Kiera: *I'll build another bridge.*

Dad: *Oooh, that's a very good idea. Ahhh, you are starting with a red brick, and now a blue brick, now a yellow one. Oooh, three bricks, that is getting very high.*

Kiera: *Oh, it's fallen over again.*

Dad: *Never mind, I thought you did a great job. Oh, you are trying again – you are very patient – I like it when you're patient.*

Dad: *Okay, we have to finish soon. So, we can build the bridge one more time, and then it's time to tidy up.*

This is an example of a parent doing really good 'Special Play' with his child. The dad does several things very well.

Descriptive commentary

He describes what Kiera is doing all the time. This way, Kiera knows that she has her dad's attention completely.

Praise

Dad gives Kiera lots of praise. He is careful to give praise for things that she finds difficult, for example, staying calm and trying again when the bridge falls down. He gives general praise too, for example, 'I do like playing with you'.

Affection

There is affection – a stroke of Kiera's hair.

Imitation

Dad mimics Kiera when she makes the train noise. Again, this subtle gesture tells the child that her parent is attending fully and approves of what she is doing.

---

[1] *The Parent/child Game: The Proven Key to a Happier Family*, Bloomsbury Publishing, New York, NY, US, pp. 278.

Preparing for ending

Dad gives Kiera a warning that their play session is about to end and links it to a concrete activity that the child can understand (building the bridge one more time). This reduces the chances of upset when the play session finishes.

Dad also avoids doing several things that are 'banished' during this type of Special Play.

No criticism

He did not make any criticism of the child. Dad may have thought that it was silly to have the dinosaur driving the train (dinosaurs didn't have trains in their day!) but he is careful not to pass this on. This play is about having a lovely, positive, friendly time.

No leading

Dad did not lead the child. Kiera was completely in charge of what was going on in the play. This is crucial for developing the child's sense of control over their world.

No testing or questions

It is very easy to start asking questions, such as 'what colour is this brick?' These are fine in ordinary play, but in this Special Play, the child should be in charge of what is happening, and should not have his/her attention distracted onto topics chosen by the parent. So, no questions, and no direct teaching are allowed. Notice that Dad did label some colours and numbers himself. This is fine, and has been shown to help children to learn without the parent asking questions.

No messages about threat and danger

Anxious parents often find themselves giving messages about danger and 'being careful' during play. For example, 'oh dear, the tower is getting really high now it's going to fall. Be careful, one of those bricks could take your eye out'.

In-session practice

Getting it wrong!

One group leader gets on the floor and tips out the bag of toys. Then, he/she invites a carefully chosen parent (someone who is not likely to strongly resist joining in the exercise, who is relatively confident and who is likely to be able to consider how the play felt and provide some fairly coherent reflections on this) to come and play with him/her. The parent is told to pretend that he/she is about 5 years old, and that the group leader is his/her parent.

The group leader then proceeds to play with the 'child' but makes every mistake in the book such as:

- asking lots of questions to the child;
- bossing the child about;
- criticising the child;
- being distracted by other things;
- trying to directly teach the child;
- competing with the child;
- giving the child lots of warning messages.

The group leader asks the 'child' what the play felt like. You should get a fairly negative response! However, some parents might be reluctant to be overly negative and you may need to ask the group for their views.

The group discusses what the group leader did wrong, and the key points are written on the flip chart/board. This should include both things to avoid and how to do things more effectively.

Getting it right!

The group leader repeats the exercise with the same 'child', but this time models doing the play well. If group leaders have not acted this type of play before, we very strongly advise a bit of practice beforehand. It's amazing how easily those little questions slip out . . . .

Ask the 'child' how this version felt, focusing on differences from the first demo.

Ask the group for their thoughts on the two versions of play, including

- how the child felt;
- who was in control;
- the emotional tone of the play;
- the effect on the child's creativity and self-expression;
- the level of conflict;
- how the parent might feel;
- any reservations parents might have about the 'getting it right' version.

Help the group reflect on how this Special Play might bolster the Seven Confident Thoughts. Play is *fundamental* to developing all of the Seven Confident Thoughts, but in particular, it helps with:

- *The world is a pretty safe place.* This play should feel very safe and reassuring for children. They can be sure that they will be safe from harm when they are with a parent who is paying such close attention to them.
- *I can cope with most things.* During play, children are always learning new skills, and they will often use play to work through emotional issues. Therefore, this play is good for helping children feel that they can cope with the world.
- *Bad things don't usually happen to me.* During this play, nothing bad will happen – the child won't even get criticised.
- *I have some control over the things that happen to me.* Children actually have very little control over their lives, so this is a difficult thought to build. Using this play makes sure that every child has at least 10 minutes a day when he/she is in total control.
- *People are pretty nice really.* This play allows the child at least 10 minutes a day that provide a guaranteed positive interaction with another person. This unconditionally positive interaction starts to build this important confident thought.
- *Other people respect me.* This can also be a difficult thought to build, but this Special Play ensures that every child gets 10 minutes a day of strong and clear messages that he/she is liked and respected.

This play is quite hard to do when you are first starting out! Most people will find this an unnatural and somewhat uncomfortable way of interacting with children on their first few attempts and children (especially slightly older ones) may ask parents 'why are you talking in that funny way?' Parents need to be know that it's a hard skill to learn, and that they shouldn't feel bad if they don't get it right the first few times. Parents should be specifically prepared for:

- accidentally asking questions;
- inadvertently reverting to old habits (e.g. criticising, taking over, etc.);
- feeling embarrassed or awkward;
- the children being unsure of what to do, especially if they are used to their parents taking a high level of control of play.

Group practice

The group leader plays the child and sits on the floor in front of the group with a set of toys. Each parent takes turn to give a brief commentary on the play. Problem solve any difficulties and ask the group to support each other. Again, normalise how challenging this type of play is at the outset. Try to get each parent to give at least one effective piece of commentary.

Identifying likely problems with Special Play

It is worth spending some time focusing on the most common difficulties that parents encounter when they first try to use Special Play.

Battles over ending the play

Because this type of play is so rewarding for children, they will often be resistant to ending the play. If this leads to tears, lengthy battles or anger, parents are less likely to persevere with daily play sessions. Preparing parents for this eventuality will help them to manage it effectively and avoid catastrophic misinterpretations of either their competence or the child's distress. Ask the group to guess how children will respond to the end of the play and then get them to problem solve how to manage this. Ideas that help to reduce parental and child distress and battles include the following:

- Expecting some resistance to end of play at first (the play was *so* much fun that child doesn't want to stop).
- Giving clear warnings about play sessions ending in a form that a child can understand (i.e. concrete and visible).
- If you say the play has to end in 1 minute, stick to it (to minimise children's future attempts to extend the sessions).
- Incorporating play into existing routines (e.g. after tea and before taking bath) so that children quickly understand that Special Play will be a daily occurrence.
- Planning another fun activity for the child following play so that the child has something to entertain them (e.g. a favourite TV programme, bath time, story time, etc.).

Finding time to play

Ask each parent to identify when in his/her day he/she will do the play. This increases the chances that parents will do it, and helps you to spot and solve any difficulties for parents in scheduling playtime.

Playing with more than one child at once

Many parents will have more than one child at home and may be concerned about how they will manage to play with each child. If possible, help parents to identify a time to play separately with each child (e.g. playing with a younger child while an older one is at school and playing with the older one after the younger one has gone to bed). Additionally, it is helpful to practice the skill of playing with two (or more) children at once. In this practice, it is essential to consider how to direct parental attention in the event of one child playing appropriately and the other behaving less well.

Home practice

- Practice Special Play for just 10 minutes, every day.
  Emphasise that this type of play takes a bit of getting used to – for both the parent and the child, but if you persevere, everyone gets the hang of it.
  - o They should start by doing it with just one child if possible. It is far more difficult with two or more children, but parents can move on to that when they have mastered doing it with one.
  - o Encourage the child to choose an activity that is interactive – i.e. not watching TV or playing a video game.
- Continue thinking about TFB.

Key messages for the session

- Adult play strengthens the parent–child bond. This builds children's confidence and independence, and is central to the success of the programme.
- This Special Play is a way of allowing children some control over their world. Feeling some control is critical to overcoming anxiety.

▶ Key Cognitions to Elicit and Challenge

- I can't play with my child.
  There may be many reasons that parents think this. They may feel embarrassed or uncomfortable playing, especially if their own parents rarely played with them, or they have never played with their own child. Alternatively, they may have experiences of their child rejecting their attempts to play with them in the past (often this is related to parents' tendency to control the play). Encourage the parents to take small steps towards playing with their child. They may need to start playing for just a couple of minutes, or with another adult helper. Help them to face their fears as they will eventually help their children to face theirs – by taking small steps and getting lots of praise and support for this.
- It is better for my child to play with other children than to play with adults.
  Children should be playing with children *and* their parents. Reinforce the messages about play being great for learning language and social skills and for enhancing the parent–child bond.
- If I let my child control the play, won't he expect to be in charge of me all the time?
  Encourage the group to reflect on what we are modelling to children when we do as they ask us during play (complying with requests and commands). Discuss how children learn by copying. Explain that children consistently become more compliant after this type of play, rather than more challenging.
- I don't like playing the games that my child plays.
  Some parents will be uncomfortable with certain toys or games that their children select. It may be helpful to help the individuals and the group consider what the reason is for their discomfort and the possibility of allowing children choices from a selection of games that parents *would* be happy to play.
- If I play with my children, they will become dependent on me.
  Reinforce the messages about adult–child play being useful for the child's learning, and for the parent–child bond. Discuss research showing that children who have a stronger bond with their parents are actually *more* independent than children who have a weaker bond. Having a safe, strong, base to roam from is very confidence-giving to children.

▶ Don't Forget . . .

- Although this is a manualised intervention, remember the unique individuals in your group. Try to think about how they will each respond to the material in this session.
- Keep drawing out 'principles' and referring back to those generated by group members in previous sessions.
- Keep giving out those stickers to model reward and so that parents have a ready supply to use at home.
- Have fun! If you have fun, so will the group members.

Condensed session plan/treatment checklist

Item/concept	Group leader	Tick when completed
Part 1		
Go over ground rules		
Feedback on home practice Thoughts, Feelings and Behaviour The Attention Rule Blame and responsibility		
Part 2		
Why is play good? It invests in the pyramid Children learn through play It builds the parent-child relationship It's not always fun for the parent		
Role play of getting it wrong Teaching Questions Criticism Competitive Distracted Taking charge		
Role play of getting it right Descriptive commentary Let the child lead No teaching No questions Lots of praise Affection Imitation		
Home practice		
Practise play 10 minutes a day Continue watching out for your TFB		
Key messages to be covered		
Adult play strengthens the parent–child bond. This builds children's confidence and independence and is central to the success of the programme		
Playing in this way gives control to children, which is excellent for anxious children		
Key cognitions to be elicited and challenged		
I can't play with my child		
It is better for my child to play with other children than to play with adults		
If I let my child control the play, won't he expect to be in charge of me all the time?		
If I play with my children, they will become dependent on me		

PLAY

This week Dr Esmeralda answers your questions about play

"Dear Dr Esmeralda,

I'm really not sure about all this play stuff you keep going on about. I don't think I should be playing with my Florence. I want her to learn to play with other children – I don't want her getting dependent on me!"

Philomena Fusspot,

Little Flossing

Dr Esmeralda replies:

Dear Philomena,

You are right. Children need to learn to play with other children. But where do they learn to do things best? That is right, at the knee of someone they love and trust. Also, in playing with you, little Florence is building a strong relationship with you. That way, when the time comes for you to ask her to do things she doesn't like, she is more likely to do it. Doing this particular sort of play is very good for making children feel important and special – and that is very good for anxious children. In fact, out of all the things we psychologists bang on about, the play is the most important – invest in it now, and you will see the benefits.

Dear Dr Esmeralda,

I love doing the play with my little Horace. He enjoys it so much and I can really see his confidence growing. But one thing worries me. This type of play gives a lot of control to children, and isn't too much control bad for anxious children?

Humphrey Honeyfoot

Toad in the Hole.

Dr Esmeralda replies:

Dear Humphrey,

I think we have to make sure that we give the control at the right times. It would be very bad to give any child control over something very important – such as deciding whether to go to school or not. But giving control over little things, like what socks to wear, what to have for pudding and so on, are really good for anxious kids. It makes them feel that they do have a say in what happens to them, and makes them feel that they can cope when difficult things crop up.

It sounds like you are doing a great job Humphrey – keep up the good work!

1

Special Play
What is Special Play?

This is the first step to you and your child working together. Playing with your child helps them to feel very special. It builds up your relationship with them and helps them want to please you. It gives you and your child the chance to spend some positive time together and forms the building blocks for working through problems.

When to do the Special Play

You need to take just 10 minutes to play together. Try to do this every day. It might be helpful to plan a time so you don't forget.

How to do the Special Play

1. Join in with your child's game or ask them to choose a game to play with you. Any toy or game will do (but not watching the television or a computer game).

2. Watch very carefully what your child is doing and comment positively so he or she knows that you are interested (give a running commentary). This is called 'attending'.

3. Imitate what your child is doing but do not take charge of the play. This shows your child that you are interested in what they are doing.

4. Ask your child what they *want* to do **but** don't ask them questions about *what* they are doing. Asking questions distracts your child from their play, and can interfere with their creativity.

5. Do not tell your child what to do during this special play. Giving them control builds up their confidence.

6. Do not try to teach your child anything. We all want our kids to do well at school, and teaching your kids new things is great. However, during this special play, it's all about having fun— forget about teaching for ten minutes.

The purpose is for you to both enjoy Special Play. When you start to play with your child in this way it may take some time for you both to get used to it so STICK AT IT!

CHAPTER FIVE

Session Three

Understanding Children's Anxiety

▶ Overview

In this session, after feedback on home practice, parents start to learn about child anxiety. A simplified cognitive behavioural explanation of child anxiety is given. This focuses on the key cognitions that are present in both the parent and the child when a child is anxious. It also focuses on the role of avoidance of fearful situations and adult modelling of anxiety.

▶ Before the Session

- Arrange room as described for Session One (Chapter Two).
- Laminate 'principles' from Session Two and stick them on the wall.
- Stick 'ground rules' from Session One on the wall.
- Stick up a large 'Seven Confident Thoughts' poster in a prominent location.
- Stick up the 'Anxiety Pyramid' poster.

▶ The Session – Part 1

- **Welcome families**
- **Feedback on home practice**

Feedback will fill most of Part 1 of the session. It should follow the general guidance on feedback on home practice that is given in Chapter Two.

Content of feedback

Feedback should be focused mostly on issues raised in Session Two, that is, Special Play. However, it is also important to keep referring back to Thoughts, Feelings and Behaviour (TFB) and The Attention Rule.

From Timid to Tiger: A Treatment Manual for Parenting the Anxious Child. By Dr Sam Cartwright-Hatton with Dr Ben Laskey, Dr Stewart Rust and Dr Deborah McNally
© 2010 John Wiley & Sons, Ltd.

Special Play

Key questions to ask:

- Who has tried Special Play?
- What did you do/play with?
- What did you say?
- Can you give me an example of a descriptive comment you used?
- How did your child react?
- Did anyone find it hard to stick to the rules?
- How did play feel for you?
- How do you think play felt for your child?

Key principles to draw out:

- Adult play strengthens the parent–child bond, building child confidence and independence; this is central to the success of the programme.
- This Special Play is a way of allowing children some control over their world. Feeling some control is critical to overcoming anxiety.
- Special Play reinforces the Seven Confident Thoughts.
- Emphasise link to The Attention Rule and that play is a form of attention.
- Play may reduce anxious and attention-seeking behaviour as children adapt to receiving attention during play instead of needing to work for it.

TFB

This was taught in Session One, and is a key concept of the programme.

The Attention Rule

This was taught in Session One, and is a key concept of the programme.

Troubleshooting feedback

The most common difficulties that are raised in this feedback session are as follows

- Parents have not done the homework (practicing Special Play for 5–10 minutes a day). Try to find out why this is so. The most common reasons and useful ways of challenging them are reprinted from Chapter Four.
  - *Battles over ending the play*
    Because this type of play is so rewarding for children they will often be resistant to ending the play. If this leads to tears, lengthy battles or anger, parents are less likely to persevere with daily play sessions. Preparing parents for this eventuality will help them to manage it effectively and avoid catastrophic misinterpretations of either their competence or the child's distress. Ask the group to guess how children will respond to the end of the play and then get them to problem solve how to manage this. Ideas that are likely to reduce parental and child distress and battles include the following.
    - Expecting some resistance to end of play at first (the play was *so* much fun that child doesn't want to stop).
    - Giving clear warnings about play sessions ending in a form that a child can understand (i.e. concrete and visible).

- Sticking consistently to agreed ending time of play (to minimise child's future attempts to extend the sessions).
- Incorporating play into existing routines (e.g. after tea and before bathtime) so that a child quickly understands that Special Play will be a daily occurrence.
- Planning another fun activity for the child following play so that the child has something to entertain them (e.g. a favourite TV programme, bath time, story time, etc.).

○ *Finding time to play*

Ask each parent to identify when in his/her day he/she will do the play. This increases the chances that parents will carry out the Special Play and enables identification and problem-solving of any difficulties for parents in scheduling playtime.

○ *Playing with more than one child at once*

Many parents will have more than one child at home and may be concerned about how they will manage to play with each child. If possible, help parents to identify a time to play separately with each child (e.g. playing with a younger child while an older one is at school and playing with the older one after the younger one has gone to bed). Additionally, it will be helpful to practice the skill of playing with two (or more) children at once. In this practice, it is essential to consider how to direct parental attention in the event of one child playing appropriately and the other behaving less well.

- Parents have negative beliefs about the play technique. The most common of these, and suggestions for challenging them, are reprinted from Chapter Four.

○ *I can't play with my child.*

There may be many reasons that parents think this way. They may feel embarrassed or uncomfortable playing, especially if their own parents rarely played with them or if they have never played with their own child. Alternatively, they may have experiences of their children rejecting their attempts to play with them in the past (often this is related to parents' tendency to control the play). Encourage the parents to take small steps towards playing with their child. They may need to start playing for just a couple of minutes, or with another adult helper. Help them to face their fears as they will eventually help their children to face theirs – by taking small steps and getting lots of praise and support for this.

○ *It is better for my child to play with other children than to play with adults.*

Children should be playing with children *and* their parents. Reinforce the messages about play being great for learning language and social skills and for enhancing the parent–child bond.

○ *If I let my child control the play, won't he expect to be in charge of me all the time?*

Encourage the group to reflect on what we are modelling to children when we do as they ask us during play (complying with requests and commands). Discuss how children learn by copying and explain that children consistently become more obedient following this type of play, rather than more challenging.

○ *I don't like playing the games that my child plays.*

Some parents will be uncomfortable with certain toys or games that their children select. It may be helpful to help the individuals and the group consider what the reason is for their discomfort and the possibility of allowing children choices from a selection of games that parents *would* be happy to play.

○ *If I play with my children, they will become dependent on me.*

Reinforce the messages about adult–child play being useful for the child's learning, and for the parent–child bond. Discuss research showing that children who have a stronger bond with their parents are actually *more* independent than children who have a weaker bond. Having a safe, strong, base to roam from is very confidence-giving to children.

The fight/flight response

As we outlined in Chapter One, the fight/flight response is key to understanding anxiety disorders. It is extremely important that parents understand the fight/flight response, and, in particular, understand that it is *not harmful* to their child.

To explain the fight/flight response, we use 'The Story of the Dinosaur and the Caveman'.

> *Once upon a time, there was a little caveman, wandering through the woods, thinking about what to have for lunch.*

Draw The Little Caveman on the whiteboard.

> *All of a sudden, round the corner, he sees an ENORMOUS . . . . . . DINOSAUR*

Draw a hungry-looking dinosaur on the whiteboard.

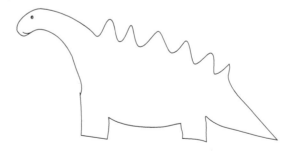

Ask the group:

- 'What is the Little Caveman thinking?' Make sure that the responses you get here are *thoughts* rather than *feelings*.
- 'What is the Little Caveman feeling?'
- 'What is the Little Caveman's behaviour?' Continue when someone offers 'he wants to run away', or similar.
- 'What does the Little Caveman's body have to do in order that he can run away really, really quickly?' Socratically elicit the following and draw them onto the Little Caveman:
  - He needs to produce lots of *adrenalin*.
  - The adrenalin makes his *heart* pump fast.

- ○ The heart pumps blood and oxygen to his *muscles* in his arms and legs.
- ○ He has to work his *lungs* hard to get in lots of oxygen.
- ○ This extra blood is drawn away from his *intestines* and sometimes from his *skin* and his *hands* and *feet*.
- ○ He has to send extra blood to his *brain* so that he can think very quickly.
- ○ All these activities make his *temperature* go up.

Next, draw a picture of a modern human being on the board.

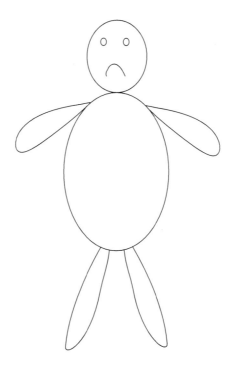

Here we have, a modern, 21st century, sophisticated, human being.

Sadly, our poor, modern, sophisticated, 21st century human being, is feeling a little scared.

Draw a sad face on the human being.

Socratically elicit from group members the physical feelings that everyone gets in their bodies when they are feeling anxious. Draw these on the picture of the 21st century human being. Try to elicit most of the following.

- Racing heart
- Tight chest
- Lump in throat
- Spinning head/dissociation/feeling faint
- Cold hands or feet
- Pale skin
- Butterflies in the stomach
- Feeling sick
- Feeling like you want to go to the toilet
- Jelly legs/shaking
- Feeling hot and sweaty.

Emphasise that we are all unique. We all get our own special subset of these. It is rare to get them all, and it might vary from time to time.

So, hmmm, does this picture of modern, 21st century, human being remind you of anything . . . ?

That's right – it looks exactly like the picture of the terrified Little Caveman who is running away from the dinosaur. Although we think we are terribly modern and sophisticated with our laptops and ipods, in fact, when it comes to being scared, we are just exactly the same as the Little Caveman. The bit of our brain that deals with being scared is exactly the same as it was 10,000 years ago. So, when we feel scared, or when our child feels scared, we act as if we have just seen a dinosaur, and our body tries to make us run away. Now, running away might not be the best way of dealing with being scared of the dentist, or of school, or of the toilet, but it is what our caveman brain tells us to do.

So, do you think that all of this stuff happening in your body can be harmful for your child? Who thinks that it isn't harmful? That's right; it's not harmful at all. Although it feels like something awful is happening to your child when he/she has the fight/flight response, in fact they are not in any danger.

Emphasise that the fight/flight response is not harmful. Point out the following:

- After having a bit of a fright, our immune charge is supercharged for a few hours, so, we are more resistant to germs and bugs.

- Sprinters use the fight/flight response to get a lightning quick start to races. You don't see many unhealthy sprinters!

- You *can't faint* during the fight/flight response. It feels as if you might faint because of the blood rushing to your brain. However, to faint, your blood pressure has to fall. During the fight/flight response, your blood pressure goes up, so you can't faint.[1]

- You *can't go mad* during the fight/flight response. It can feel as if you are going mad because of the rush of blood to the head, and the very rapid and frightening thought processes. Emphasise that the fight/flight response is *completely normal* and is not a sign of madness.

It is critically important that parents understand that the strange physical sensations their child experiences when frightened are harmless. If parents have any residual concerns that these are signs of illness or damage, then they will find it difficult to follow subsequent stages of the programme.

The role of avoidance

As outlined in Chapter One, avoidance is the key behavioural factor in maintaining anxiety. Briefly, if we avoid things that we are frightened of, we do not get the opportunity to find out that they are harmless. We also miss out on opportunities to learn new coping skills. Finally, the longer we avoid, the bigger the fear gets. These are important concepts to get across to parents. We do this by telling them 'The Story of the Dragon in the Mountain'.

Right, I want to tell you a little story. We tell this to all of the children that we see, and I want to tell it to you too. Are you sitting comfortably? Then I shall begin.

Once upon a time, a long, long, time ago, there was a little tribe of villagers. These villagers were poor, but they were happy, for they lived at the bottom of a huge volcano. And, as you know, volcanoes are very lush and fertile places. So, these villagers had the life of Riley! They would wake up in the morning, and go up the mountain to collect a wonderful feast. All sorts of things grew on this volcano – peach trees, chocolate Hobnob bushes . . . and the villagers would fill their baskets, eat their fill, and then sleep it off in the afternoon sun. Lovely! Then one day, something terrifying happened. There was a storm. But the villagers hadn't seen a storm before, and this was no ordinary storm. The thunder crashed and the rain lashed the village. The lightning flashed and silhouetted the volcano against the black night sky. The villagers were terrified! 'What is happening?' they said. 'What is happening to our mountain?' Just then, one of the village elders spoke up 'Ahhh, it is the dog in the mountain. He is angry with us for taking his food'. There were gasps of horror from the villagers as they huddled together out of fear and cold.

---

[1] Some people can faint when they see blood or if they have an injection or blood test. However, if this has not yet happened to anyone's child, it is unlikely that they have this problem. For further information on this fairly uncommon condition, readers are referred to Ost, L.G. and Sterner, U. (1987) Applied tension: A specific behavioral method for treatment of blood phobia. *Behaviour Research and Therapy*, 25 (1), 25–9.

The next day, the sun rose, and it was time for the villagers to go up the volcano to collect their food … but no one dared go up the mountain …. And the next day came, and still no one would dare go up the mountain, and the next week came, and the next month came, and the next year came, and still, no one dared go up the mountain.

*As the years went by, the villagers scraped a living on the thin soils around the volcano. Life was not easy, but they survived, on a meagre diet of sprouts and goats cheese (insert foods group leaders finds repulsive, these are just ours). And, as is the way with these things, as the years went by, the rumours about the volcano grew and grew. Soon, it was not a dog in the mountain, but a **lion** in the mountain. And then, it stopped being a lion in the mountain, and became a **dragon** in the mountain. And, eventually, it stopped being a dragon in the mountain, and became a **fire-breathing, baby-eating, dragon in the mountain**, and there was **no way** that anyone was going up there to get food.*

Then, one year, the unthinkable happened. The rains didn't come, and the crops failed. The villagers had nothing to eat, and soon they were on the verge of starvation. They called a village meeting, to decide what they should do.

So, what should they do?

Someone will say 'go up the mountain to get food'.

(Exasperated voice) *'But they can't go up the mountain. There's a dragon in the mountain … isn't there … ?'*

Someone will say 'Of course not.'

So, how do they find out that there is really no dragon in the mountain?

Socratically elicit the idea that they *have* to go up the mountain, to find out that there really is no dragon.

So, that is exactly what the villagers decided. They made one of the elders go up the mountain, to see if there really was a dragon.

*So, the old man started walking up the mountain. His legs were shaky, but he kept walking up the mountain. His chest was tight, he felt that he might faint, but still he walked, up, and up the mountain (group leader acts this out). And soon, he reached the top … of … the … mountain (we usually climb on a chair). (terrified voice) But just as he reached the top of the mountain, there was a **ginormous** ….*

(Pause for suspense, and then group leader jumps off chair).

Oh how old are you lot? There's no such thing as dragons. He filled his baskets with food, and climbed back down the mountain where they all had an enormous feast and lived happily ever after.

So, when we tell this story to anxious children, what is our message?

Socratically elicit the idea that if you have a fear, you have to go 'up the mountain'. You have to 'test it out'.

Socratically elicit the idea that if you don't test out a fear as soon as possible, it gets bigger and bigger and bigger until it is the size of a terrifying dragon.

Anxiety TFB

We have already covered the Thoughts, Feelings and Behaviour concept, but we go over it again, emphasising its role in anxiety.

The group leaders volunteer something that they are a bit scared of. For us, in no particular order, it is blood, snakes, crustacea (!) and moths. Volunteering this information about ourselves makes it easier for group members to disclose their own fears. We then choose one of the group's fears (preferably one that is not so deeply held that discussing it will send the person screaming from the room), and we draw up a TFB cycle for that fear.

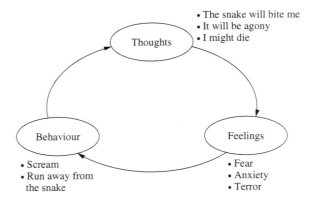

Explain that, as always, scary thoughts, such as 'the snake might bite me and I will die', lead to feelings of fear and anxiety. These feelings lead us to want to run away from the snake. Running away means that we never go 'up that mountain'. So, we never find out that the vast majority of snakes (in this country), and as long as you don't torment them, are perfectly harmless.

At this point, we add an 'avoidance cycle' onto the TFB drawing.

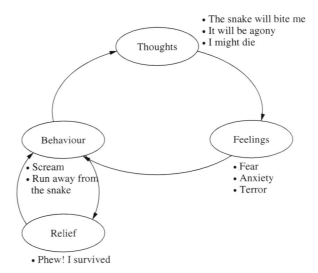

Explain that avoiding things we are scared of becomes a very ingrained behaviour, and one that is difficult to break. This is because when we escape from our fear, we experience a powerful feeling of relief. This rewards our avoidance behaviour, and increases the odds that we will avoid the next time we encounter our fear.

Going up the mountain – to push or not to push . . . ?

The purpose of this exercise is to get parents to think about pushing their own child to go 'up the mountain' and test out their fears. Pushing their child to face deeply held fears is one of the toughest things that we ask parents to do on this course. Without proper preparation, many find it impossible to do. So, before we begin to teach parents how to do this, we lay the cognitive groundwork. In other words, we make sure that they are psychologically prepared for the step that we are about to ask them to take.

We have found that parents are much more likely to help their children test out their fears if all of their own worries and concerns about doing this have first been heard and addressed. In this exercise, we use a 'pros and cons' exercise to allow parents to voice their fears.

A 2 × 2 table is drawn on the board.

	Pushing	Not pushing
Pros		
Cons		

Explain that this exercise is looking at the pros and cons of encouraging (pushing) your child to face his/her fears. The group leaders then start to fill in the boxes, using information from the group. We always do them in the following order.

Pros of not pushing
Ask parents about the benefits if they didn't bother pushing their child.

- *It will be easier to not bother* (fair point!).
- *My child won't get upset.*
- *I won't get upset.*
- *It will be less time and hassle for the whole family.*

Pros of pushing
Ask parents about the benefits of pushing their child. Socratically elicit the following:

- *My child might get more confident.*
- *My child will have a better life.*
- *My child will feel good about themselves.*
- *It will boost the Seven Confident Thoughts.*
- *I will feel great as a parent.*
- *Once it's done, family life will be easier.*
- *My child will have learnt a useful life-skill.*

Cons of pushing
Ask parents to share their worries about pushing their children to face their fears.

- *It could harm my child.* If you get this one, reassure parents that you will teach them how to do this very carefully, so that they will not do any harm.
- *It could go wrong.* Explain that you will teach parents how to do it to maximise the chances of success, but if it goes wrong, it's not the end of the world, and you will help them to sort it out.

- My child will hate me. It is worth acknowledging that the child might be angry with the parent. Discuss whether this is likely to be long or short term.
- I will get very upset. Acknowledge that this is a possibility. Help parents rehearse what they can say to themselves if they get upset.
- It will be a hassle. Acknowledge that this could be true.

Cons of not pushing

Ask parents to think about the risks of not pushing their children to face their fears. Socratically elicit the following:

- My child won't get any better.
- My child might get worse – he/she may struggle to find a good job, a girlfriend, to leave home ...
- I might feel that I've missed a chance to help my child.

We then take a vote on whether we think we should push or not push our children to face their fears. We always get a unanimous 'push' vote. But if you do not, it is worth spending extra time working with any parents who voted 'not push' as it is likely that they will struggle with the remainder of the programme.

It is now very important to emphasise that you have not yet given parents the tools to push their child. Parents should not rush home and start pushing their child to face their fears. Ask parents to hold on for one more week, as they will be learning about facing fears in the next session.

Parental modelling of anxiety

As discussed in Chapter One, it is now known that a large proportion of anxiety is learnt. The following exercises are aimed at getting parents to think about how they might be teaching their child to be anxious. It is obviously very important that this is done in a sympathetic and non-blaming manner. For this reason, we use a lot of humour and silliness in this section.

Kids copy their parents? Never ...!

To begin, the group leaders divulge something embarrassing that their child has done as a direct result of copying them. Alternatively, you could disclose something embarrassing that you did as a child, which you learnt from a parent. The funnier and more embarrassing it is, the better. For example, one of us discloses that, mimicking a house-proud mother at the age of five, she emerged from a friend's bathroom and announced 'you are right Mummy, that toilet *is* disgusting ...'.

At this point, we usually find that group members are falling over themselves to offer similar, and often hilarious anecdotes. The message that should be drawn from this fun is that children copy their parents' behaviour.

Modelling vignettes

These exercises are not for the shy and retiring group leader. It is best left to someone who is prepared to make a bit of a fool of themselves (not prepared to make a bit of a fool of yourself – why are you running a parents' group?).

'The Dentist'

> *OK, I want you all to imagine that you are about five years of age, and I am your Mum/Dad.*

(Wailing, slightly histrionic tones and much overreacting should be involved) *Oh crikey, I can't believe I've got to go the dentist again. I flipping hate the dentist. It hurt like hell last time.*

And I hate that ruddy dentist. Honestly, I swear he enjoys hurting people – he's a psychopath. And that nurse, she's a cow! Standing there, smiling at me saying 'are yer alriiiight?' Of course I'm not alright; I'm at the effing dentist. Oh God, I can't do it . . . Right, I'm not going (mimes dialling the phone). *Hello, is that the dentists? I'm not coming* (mimes slamming the phone down). (Shouts to unseen person offstage) *Derek, where's the gin . . . ?*

Follow-up questions:

- *OK, you are five years old. You've never been to the dentist. You've never even heard of the dentist. What are you thinking about the dentist right now?*
- *What have you learnt about how you cope with anxiety?* (That you should avoid the frightening stimulus.)
- *What else have you learnt?* (Mime drinking gin from the bottle.) (That you can use alcohol to manage anxiety.)
- *How will you react when someone tries to make you go to the dentist next week?*
- *How does all of this feed into the Seven Confident Thoughts?*

'The Wedding'

> *OK, you are all about five years old, and I'm your Mum/Dad. We are in the car, going to a wedding (it's a people carrier).*

(In nagging, agitated voice) *Come on Derek, get a move on, I'm not being late again, not like last time. All those people turning round and staring at us walking in late. And please try to take us to the right church this time. And you lot in the back there, you'd better be on your best behaviour. I'm not having a repeat performance of last time; people must have thought you were dragged up. And . . . good grief* (walks up to a parent and wipes imaginary smudge off shoulder) *look at the state of you already! What will people think of me? And you* (picks another parent) *– we'll have no more of* **that** *behaviour. Yes,* **that** *behaviour – you know what I'm talking about. Oh God, now I've got one of my heads coming on. Come on Derek, get a move on, and when we get there, I think we'll just stay for one drink, so people don't think we're being off, and then we'll go home. Make mine a double . . . .*

Follow-up questions:

- *You were looking forward to a fun family party. What are you thinking now?*
- *What will other people be thinking about you?* (They will be judging you, closely examining your appearance and behaviour.)
- *How do you cope if you feel socially anxious?* (Drink alcohol and leave asap.)
- *How does this feed into the Seven Confident Thoughts?*

It is important to emphasise that you do not think that any of your group members would be this daft, but that you just wanted to do something memorable to remind people that children often copy our behaviour, and that includes our anxious behaviour.

We find it helpful to remind parents that anxious children have an extra body part that other children do not have. This is their stress radar, and if you part their hair, and look very carefully, you can see it sticking up about three feet out of their heads. Children who have this radar can detect stress, fear, worry and potential danger at a distance of up to 1000 paces, whereas average children can only detect it if it's staring them in the face. So, if you are the parent of one of these children, you have to be extra-super careful not to model anxiety to your kids. So, how on earth do you do this . . . ?

Zipper Mouth, Botox Face and the Oscar-Winning Performance

Once parents have learnt to identify the things that they do and say that might pass their anxiety to their children, you need to give them some techniques to help manage this.

We use three highly scientific techniques to achieve this.

Zipper Mouth

Remember 'Zippy' from Rainbow? The irritating orange space alien (we think that's what he was) from British 1970s kids TV. Who else lived in daily hope that Geoffrey would finally see red and shut the zip on his mouth?

If you feel something that is scary, or frightening, or that will undermine all of your hard work, coming out of your mouth, it's time to implement zipper-mouth. Take the zip firmly in your right hand, and zip it completely shut. Not to be re-opened until the moment has passed, or you are in danger of starving to death.

Botox Face

This is a slightly more advanced technique, and involves pretending that you are someone who has had way too much Botox (group leader adopts frozen, neutral, preferably slightly bizarre facial expression). When you use this technique in conjunction with zipper mouth, not only can you not say anything scary, but you can't even give away the fact that you are scared with your facial expression.

Oscar-Winning Performance

This is really only for the advanced practitioner, and can take many years of dedicated training to perfect. It involves adopting a happy, relaxed facial expression, in the face of actual bodily terror (Group leader models the Oscar-Winning Performance – deep breath, shoulders back, huge rictus grin and off you go).

Of course, these are not quite the highly specialised, scientific techniques that we have painted them as. However, they do operate as another entertaining and memorable way of pushing home the message that children pick up on their parents' fears from hearing what they say, watching what they do and even just looking at their facial expressions.

Compensating

In many cases, the best outcome for a child would come about if the parent sought help for his/her own anxiety (i.e. from another adult, not from the child). Indeed, where a clear parental anxiety disorder becomes apparent, that parent would be discretely encouraged and supported to access treatment for himself/herself. When that is not possible, the parent is encouraged to use techniques, such as zipper mouth and Botox Face, to avoid passing on his/her anxiety to the child. However, there are other things that a family can do to protect a child when one of the parents has a marked fear or phobia. Therefore, we talk to the group about 'compensating'. This means that when a parent has a marked fear of a particular stimulus, he/she ensures that the child gets lots of extra opportunities to have positive experiences of that stimulus. So, for example, if a parent is afraid of spiders, we would ask him/her to find someone else who is happy to play with spiders with the child. That person could be anyone, but ideally they should:

- be very confident with the stimulus (e.g. totally confident with spiders – happy for spiders to climb all over them);

- have a good relationship with the child. Ideally, this would be someone that child looks up to a bit, such as the other parent, a big sister, favourite aunty and so on.

It is probably best if the fearful parent stays well out of the way while the compensation is taking place, to avoid unintentionally transmitting of fear information.

The person doing the compensation doesn't have to do anything special, but just play with the child and the stimulus for a few minutes. If possible, this should happen on a number of occasions.

Likewise, if a parent isn't afraid of an object, but of certain situations, like large social occasions, there is a risk that the child doesn't get much opportunity to experience those situations, and is at increased risk of developing a fear of it. The parent should encourage the child to enter the situation that they dislike (e.g. arrange for the child to go to lots of parties, etc).

Home practice

- Continue Special Play for around 10 minutes a day.
- Keep thinking about your TFB.
- Keep thinking about your child's TFB.
- Plan some compensation for your child, if you have a fear that might get passed on.

Key messages for the session

- Children copy their parents' anxious behaviours and their confident behaviours.
- The fight/flight response is not dangerous. It cannot harm your child in any way.
- Compensating – for example, if you are shy, make sure your kids get lots of socialising elsewhere.

▶ Key Cognitions to Elicit and Challenge

- My child looks so ill when he/she is anxious, I'm sure it really is bad for him/her.
- I can't push my child to do things he/she is scared of – it would feel so cruel.
- If I push my child to do things he/she is scared of, he/she will hate me.

▶ Don't Forget . . .

- Although this is a manualised intervention, remember the unique individuals in your group. Try to think about how they will each respond to the material in this session.
- Keep drawing out 'principles' and referring back to those generated by group members in previous sessions.
- Keep giving out those stickers to model reward and so that parents have a ready supply to use at home.
- Have fun! If you have fun, so will the group members.

Condensed session plan/treatment checklist

Item/concept	Group leader	Tick when completed
Part 1		
Feedback on home practice Special Play Thoughts, Feelings and Behaviour The Attention Rule		
Part 2		
Fight/flight response The Caveman and the Dinosaur		
The role of avoidance in anxiety The Story of the Dragon in the Mountain		
Anxiety TFB		
To push or not to push		
Parental modelling of anxiety 'The Dentist' vignette 'The Wedding' vignette		
Zipper mouth/Botox Face/The Oscar-Winning Performance		
Compensating		
Home practice Continue Special Play for around 10 minutes a day Keep thinking about your TFB Keep thinking about your child's TFB Plan some compensating for your child, if you have a fear that might get passed on		
Key messages to be covered		
Modelling fear, confidence and coping are very important		
Faking confidence when you are feeling anxious in front of your child		
Compensating – for example, if you are shy, make sure your kids get lots of socialising elsewhere		
Key cognitions to be elicited and challenged		
My children look so ill when they are anxious, I'm sure it really is bad for them		
I can't push my children to do things they are scared of – it would feel so cruel		
If I push my children to do things they are scared of, they will hate me		

Welcome to Session 3

FEAR AND ANXIETY

This week, Dr Esmeralda answers your questions on pushing an anxious child.

"Dear Dr Esmeralda,

My Rodney is afraid of every-thing. Last night, on a trip to the circus, he was nearly scared out of his skin by a piece of candyfloss! He was so upset that we just went home. I know I should push him to do things that he feels a bit scared of, but I just feel so sorry for him. Dr Esmeralda, is there any other way?"

Jelena Jellybeen,

Khartoon.

Dr Esmeralda replies:

Dear Jelena,

I do love to hear from caring parents who really think how things make their children feel. But Jelena, I'm afraid you have a stark choice to make. You can protect little Rodney from all the scary things in the world if you want, and he might like that now. But look to the future my dear. What will Rodney be like when you are not there to protect him? How will he cope in a world where everything is scary? How will he manage in a job? How will he manage bringing up his own little ones? Also Jelena, what will your Rodney think of himself when he grows up? We want our children to grow up knowing that they can cope with what the world throws at them. If your Rodney knows that he can't even cope with candyfloss, will he have the strong self-esteem that every mother wants for her child? Will he feel able to cope with new things and scary things? I think you know the answer to your question Jelena. He will thank you for it...I promise.

"Dear Dr Esmeralda,

It is such a big bad world out there. I love my darling Simperella so much, and I can't bear the thought of her getting hurt. I think all the other parents are terrible – letting their children roam around the cul de sac after school, letting them sleepover at neighbours' houses! Honestly, any-thing could happen. I am seriously considering calling the NSPCC about these dreadful families, and would ap-preciate your advice"

Wanda Windbag,

Over Peover.

Dr Esmeralda replies:

Dear Wanda,

You clearly care for your little Simperella a great deal. So I would make this plea to your heart. In the words of the great Sting song, "If you love somebody, set them free..." The world can be a dangerous place, but if your child is to grow up feeling confident and brave, then she needs to know that mostly it is safe. You need to make situations where your child can learn how good she is at coping on her own. By playing out on her own, and by having safe sleepovers with trusted friends, she is learning that she can cope. She is learning skills for making friends and for looking after herself. No parent can teach a child all of this on their own - not even a fantastic one. So, the best parents provide outside opportunities where their chil-dren can learn about the outside world. I'm sure you want the best for your little girl Wanda, so go on, send her outside now!

1

All About Fear and Anxiety

1 When we are anxious about something, we can get all sorts of funny feelings in our bodies – shaking, feeling sick, wobbly legs, blurred vision, feeling like we can't breathe, can't swallow, feeling dizzy, tight chest, looking pale, and many more.

2 These feelings feel horrible, but in fact they are *completely* harmless.

3 These feelings are just our body getting ready to escape from some thing that we are scared of.

4 If your child gets these feelings, be very calm and confident, and tell them it is OK and that the feelings will go away in a bit.

5 Even if you are really alarmed by the feelings that your child is having in their body, DON'T LET ON!!! If you look upset, your child will think there *really is* something to worry about!

6 If children avoid things that they are scared of, they never get used to them, and they never learn that they *can* cope with them. Remember, if we avoid things, the dragon just gets bigger!

7 Kids can learn to be afraid of things just by watching us be scared. If you are scared or worried by something, try to cope well, for the sake of your kids. Otherwise, just try to cover your fear up really well!

Session Four

Using Praise to Build Children's Confidence

▶ Overview

In this session, after feedback on home practice, we move on to deliberate shaping of children's brave and confident behaviour through positive attention. To introduce this we begin by reviewing The Attention Rule. We focus on the idea that if a behaviour gets plenty of attention (e.g. praise), that behaviour will be strengthened, that is, happens more often, for longer and more intensely. We then turn our attention to 'Stairway to Bravery' – the use of hierarchies for tackling fears and phobias.

▶ Before the Session

- Arrange the room as described in Chapter Two.
- Laminate 'principles' from Session Three and stick them on the wall.
- Stick 'ground rules' from Session One on the wall.
- Stick up a large 'Seven Confident Thoughts' poster in a prominent location.
- Stick up the 'Anxiety Pyramid' poster.

▶ The Session – Part 1

- **Welcome families**
- **Feedback on home practice**

Feedback will fill most of Part 1 of the session. It should follow the general guidance on feedback on home practice that is given in Chapter Two.

Content of feedback

Feedback should be focused mostly on issues raised in Sessions Two and Three, that is, Special Play and Anxiety Education. However, it is also important to keep referring back to the Seven Confident Thoughts, Thoughts, Feelings and Behaviour (TFB) and The Attention Rule.

From Timid to Tiger: A Treatment Manual for Parenting the Anxious Child. By Dr Sam Cartwright-Hatton with Dr Ben Laskey, Dr Stewart Rust and Dr Deborah McNally
© 2010 John Wiley & Sons, Ltd.

Anxiety education

Since few new skills were taught in Session Three (the focus was on education about the fight/flight response and avoidance), we usually just check that the key principles have been internalised.

- Children copy their parents' anxious behaviours and their confident behaviours.
- The fight/flight response is not dangerous. It cannot harm your child in any way.

Compensating

Has anyone done any compensating for their own anxiety?

- What did you do?
- Who did it?
- How did it go?
- Has anyone planned any compensating?
- What have you got planned?
- Who will do it?

Special Play

See Chapter Four for feedback on Special Play.

TFB and attention

Remember to also refer back to TFB and The Attention Rule as much as possible.

▶ The Session – Part 2

As outlined in Chapter One, praise is integral to building confidence in a child. Receiving plenty of frequent, high-quality praise for behaviours that the child is already good at, and for behaviours that they are working on, is crucial for developing the Seven Confident Thoughts (7CTs). Praise builds all of the 7CTs, but in particular, it is great for: *People are pretty nice really; other people respect me;* and for *I have some control over the things that happen to me.* This third confident thought may not be as obvious as the first two, but if you think about it, a child who has learnt exactly how to get plenty of positive attention from her parents is a child who has some wonderful control over what happens to her.

Using praise

We begin by rehearsing the Attention Rule from Session One:

Group leaders:	*What do children want more than anything in the whole world . . . ?*
Group:	*Attention.*
Group leaders:	*When do they want it . . . ?*
Group:	*Now.*
Group leaders:	*Who do they want it from?*
Group:	*Us!*

The Attention Rule is now expanded to include the idea that whenever a behaviour gets some attention, that behaviour is strengthened (happens more often and more intensely) – refer back to any principles elicited from homework feedback that highlight this and give credit to the originators (*As we know from Bob's principle: when we give attention to a behaviour it happens again* ...). Elicit the idea that praise is an especially powerful form of attention and one that we can use in a targeted way to increase the frequency of behaviours we want to see more of. So, we can use praise to get more *good* behaviours, and crucially, more *confident* behaviours.

However, to get the most out of praise, there are a number of key things to remember:

- *Focus on what you want more of, not what you want less of.*
  This is a very common mistake. Parents decide to use praise for behaviours that they want less of, for example, 'not fighting with your brother'. Ask the group what is wrong with this. The problem is, it is impossible to spot and praise behaviours that do not happen. So, this needs to be turned round, so that parents are praising for, for example, 'playing nicely with your brother'.

- *Give praise as often as possible.*
  Give praise whenever you see a behaviour you like. For anxious kids, parents should be watching out for both *good* behaviours (e.g. doing homework, tidying up toys, playing nicely with sister) and also *confident* behaviours (e.g. stroking next door's dog, going to the toilet alone, saying hello to an unfamiliar shopkeeper).

- *Do not wait for perfection.*
  Many anxious children are perfectionists, as also are the parents of many. Parents often think that they should not praise attempts at new behaviour that fall short of perfection. However, if a difficult new behaviour is to be mastered, parents really need to praise any little step in the right direction.

- *Give praise straight away.*
  Ask parents when praise should be given: *Tomorrow, next Tuesday, a week on Friday...?* Of course, praise should be given as soon as possible after the child has done the desired behaviour. The younger the child is, the more important this is. If the praise is given too late, the child will have forgotten what behaviour it was for, and it will lose its potency.

- *Sound really positive when giving praise.*
  We usually demonstrate this by giving a parent some nice praise (e.g. *Thanks for coming today Jon, I know you're really busy, so I do appreciate it*) but we give it in a really flat, bored voice, with a hangdog facial expression. We ask parents what was wrong with this praise, and get someone to show us how it should have been done.

- *Use Specific Labelled Praise.*
  We give a parent a piece of really general praise: *Thanks Jayne, that was really brilliant* and ask what was wrong with this. The problem with this praise, though very nice, is that the child doesn't know what behaviour he/she is being praised for. If the children don't know what behaviour they are being praised for, then they won't know which behaviour they need to do in order to get praise next time. For example, the parent could be praising the child for playing quietly with his sister, but he thinks that he is being praised for the lovely drawing that he has just done on the wallpaper.... So, everyone needs to learn to use Specific Labelled Praise.

- *Don't follow praise with a criticism.*
  We demonstrate this by giving a parent (choose a confident one!) some praise (e.g. *You look nice today Cheryl, I really like your outfit*) and then follow it up by a criticism (e.g. *It's a pity you can't always make the effort...*). It's always worth considering which parent is likely to be robust enough to accept being the target of this kind of comment with a smile. We ask the innocent victim of this slur to say what was wrong with the praise. Also, we ask which bit of the praise she will remember. Of course, the bit she will remember is the criticism at the end. So, this does not work well as a praise and might actually stop a child from trying the good/brave behaviour again. We talk about times

when parents do this in real life, for example, *you've been so brave . . . you see what you can do when you try . . . why don't you always do that?*

Other issues to cover:

- Accepting praise.
  Children need to learn to be able to accept praise themselves. Many anxious children find this quite difficult, particularly if they are not used to receiving it. One way of learning this is to see their parents accepting praise. We teach this idea by modelling a parent who is very poor at accepting a complement on her/his new blouse/top:
  (Looking awkward and embarrassed) *What, this old thing? Ooooh, nooo, I've had it for ages. It's only from Primark.*
  Although this is a very British, modest response, there is also a risk that it makes the person who gave the praise uncomfortable, and less likely to give praise again in the future. Also, if seen by a child, it can teach that child to reject praise, which is not something that we want to encourage.
  We then model accepting praise in a more confident and open way:
  (Big smile) *Thank you very much.*
  Some children do react with real discomfort when their parents begin piling on the praise. It is tempting for these parents to give up: *He doesn't like it, so I don't see the point.* In our experience, all children do eventually start to appreciate the praise, but if they are not used it, it can take time. These parents need extra support and encouragement to keep going, and need reassurance that although their efforts appear to have been rebuffed, they will still be doing good, and they should hang in there.
- Link praise to the Seven Confident Thoughts.
  Get the group to discuss which of the Seven Confident Thoughts are bolstered by using this sort of praise. Praise is actually good for all of the 7CTs but is particularly good for: *People are pretty nice really, Other people respect me, I have some control over the things that happen to me, Bad things don't usually happen to me.*
- Consider reviewing some examples of effective and less effective praise to check learning if there is time at the end of the session. These can be written up on flipchart or handed out on paper. Parents could be encouraged to discuss in pairs/small groups and then feedback.

Praise worksheet

Take a look at the handout for Session Four. You will see that there is a space for parents to write down:

- *Things that their child is already quite good at.* This is so that parents have ready access to some behaviours that they can easily and frequently practise praising.
- *Confident behaviours that they would like to see more of.* This is so that parents have a ready prepared list of confident behaviours to praise.
- *Good behaviours that they would like to see more of.* This is so that parents have a ready prepared list of good behaviours to praise.

Give the group members a few minutes to fill these sections in. We find that if parents go away with a plan of the behaviours that they are going to praise, they are more likely to actually do it. You may consider asking parents to discuss their plans with their neighbour or other group members, or to feedback to the group.

Troubleshooting praise

Parents are often keen to get going on the praise, but there are some problematic cognitions that can get in the way. It's worth looking out for them, and asking plenty of general questions, such as:

Does anyone have any worries about doing this kind of praise?
Has anyone got any doubts about using more praise?

A list of the most frequent and troublesome cognitions, along with some suggested responses, is given below (Key Cognitions to Elicit and Challenge).

Stairway to bravery

It is very rare that any of us masters a complex new behaviour without considerable effort, practice and support. This is particularly true for behaviours that we find frightening. We start this section by harking back to the 'Dragon and the Mountain' story, to remind parents of the need to push children to test out their fears. Then follows a discussion of how schoolchildren are taught to dive into a swimming pool:

OK, who remembers learning to dive into a swimming pool at school? (About two thirds of parents seem to have experience of this).

So, how did they teach you this new skill? Did they just grab you by the ankles and drop you in the deep end?

No, that's right, they started you off just sitting on the edge of the pool, with your legs in the water, and sort of flopping in. (Mimic sitting on the edge of a pool and sort of flopping in.)

What did they get you to do when you had mastered that?

Yes, they got you to crouch down low on the edge of the pool, and sort of flop in. (Mimic crouching low on edge of pool and flopping in.)

And then what next?

Yes, they got you to crouch again, but a bit higher up, and then flop in. And then, a bit higher, and a bit higher, and a bit higher, until eventually you could dive in from standing upright. (Mimic these actions.)

And what if they wanted you to learn to dive off a diving board? Did they just take you up to the highest board, and make you dive off it? No, that's right, you started on the lowest board and work up to the highest one, and they might get you to jump first, before you dived off.

We then explain that learning any scary new behaviour is *exactly* the same as learning to dive into a pool. You have to break it into plenty of tiny steps, and master them one by one.

To demonstrate, we get the group to brainstorm how you would break a simple phobia into steps.

We usually pick a fear that someone's child is presenting with, and we try to choose someone who will particularly benefit from the group's input. However, it is also important to pick something fairly simple, such as an animal phobia or a fear of a very specific situation.

We then teach the steps in creating a 'Stairway to Bravery' as follows:

- At the very bottom of the page (or whiteboard) write down what the child can *just about* do now. For instance, in our example, the child might be able to go to the toilet with the mother standing in the room.
- At the very top of the page (or whiteboard) write the ultimate goal for the child. This should be fairly ambitious. For instance in our example, it might be for the child to be able to go to the toilet totally on his own, with the mother downstairs and out of the way.

- Fill in the steps in between. Start at the bottom and work up. It doesn't matter how many steps there are. There could be 3 or 33, although in reality, most 'Stairways to Bravery' have about 6 to 10 steps.

- There are various ways of making the steps successively harder. For instance, in our toilet example, the mother could move further and further away from the child. Alternatively, the child could spend longer periods of time alone in the toilet before the mother came in. Be creative and mix it up a bit!

- Once a preliminary stairway has been made, teach parents how to implement it. The rules for this are:

  o Explain to the child what you are doing – get them involved in planning the stairway and the rewards, if possible.

  o Start on the bottom step. This should be pretty easy, as this should be something that the child can already just about do. This ensures that the child has an early experience of success with the stairway, and quickly and painlessly becomes familiar with its workings.

  o The child should get *tons* of praise from parents for each attempt at a step, even if it doesn't go particularly well. Every time they manage a step, they should also get a small reward. (These should have been planned in advance and should be given as soon as possible. See also Chapter Seven for rules on rewards!)

  o Repeat that step, several times if necessary, until the child is really pretty comfortable with it, before moving on to the next step.

  o When you move up a step, pay attention to how the first attempt goes. If it goes really badly, consider making the step a bit easier. It's completely normal to end up tweaking the stairway as you go along. Break down a step on your 'stairway' to demonstrate to parents how this might be achieved.

  o Help parents to consider when the best time to attempt new steps is likely to be – for example, when the child is in a good frame of mind, not when he/she is tired, hungry, or in a bad mood. Help parents also to consider the impact of their own state of mind here on the process. For example, if they are really tired from a long day at work and feeling a bit irritable then they may struggle to be tolerant of their child's distress and supportive of the child's (possibly limited) efforts.

We then ask parents to spend 10 minutes in session planning a 'Stairway to Bravery' for their child. Circulate and Socratically help parents to problem solve any obstacles they encounter. Consider asking parents to share their stairways with one another or with the group.

We ask parents to take their stairway home and negotiate starting using it with their child. Although the stairway was mainly planned in the session, we have found that the best outcomes arise when parents, at least in part, negotiate the stairway with children. If this is not possible because the child is too young, or too unmotivated to engage with the process, then they should at least be encouraged to negotiate the rewards that will come with each step.

Home practice

- Practise using praise for good behaviours.
- Practise using praise for confident behaviours.
- Begin 'Stairway to Bravery'.
- Continue Special Play for 5–10 minutes per day.
- Keep thinking about your TFB.
- Carry on doing 'compensation', if needed.

Key messages for the session

- Using Specific Labelled Praise increases *good* behaviours and *confident* behaviours.
- Parents should model accepting praise.
- It is not possible to praise a child too much, especially when they are taking on a new challenge or learning a new behaviour.
- New behaviours, especially new coping behaviours, need to be broken down into little steps, and learnt bit by bit.

▶ Key Cognitions to Elicit and Challenge

- If I praise my children all the time, they'll think they can get away with anything.
  Parents often worry that if they praise their children too much, they will get spoilt. We reassure parents that there is no such thing as too much of this type of praise. Children can become spoilt if they get plenty of praise but not enough limit setting, but praise in itself can do nothing but good.

- I can't praise my child when I am angry.
  This is very honest. It is extremely difficult to praise one behaviour when you are very upset about other things that the child is doing. Revisit The Attention Rule here. 'What will happen if we give attention to the behaviour that makes us angry?' However, parents should be encouraged to use their skills of Botox Face and Oscar-Winning Performance (learnt in Session Three) to praise the behaviour and cover up their anger. Remember, if the good behaviour gets praise, the child will divert more energy into the good behaviour, and will have less time and energy for the behaviours that you don't like. If you don't praise good and brave behaviour when you see it, you might not get the chance again.

- I do not want to praise my children all the time – the world's not like that. They need to get used to the big bad world.
  This session should refer, frequently, to the Seven Confident Thoughts. If children are to become confident, successful adults, they need to believe that the world usually is a fair, safe place. Ask the parents whether it is possible for a child who believes in a big, bad world, to ever be a truly confident person?

- My child should not have to be praised for being 'brave'.
  Parents are often frustrated that their child cannot do things that may be normal for other children of the same age. If this frustration spills over, and they cannot praise their child for small steps towards their goals, then these goals are unlikely to be achieved. We talk to parents about how famous artists achieved their success. Did their parents wait until they were producing masterpieces before they praised them? Of course not; children need to be praised for the sticky, blotchy things that they bring home from nursery. This way, their confidence grows, and only then can they take further steps towards success. This is the same for any new behaviour. Indeed, it's particularly important that parents praise behaviours that their children are struggling with.

- My child should not have to be praised for behaving.
  As above.

▶ Don't Forget . . . . .

- Although this is a manualised intervention, remember the unique individuals in your group. Try to think about how they will each respond to the material in this session.

- Keep drawing out 'principles' and referring back to those generated by group members in previous sessions.
- Keep giving out those stickers to model reward and so that parents have a ready supply to use at home.
- Have fun! If you have fun, so will the group members.

Condensed session plan/treatment checklist

Item/concept	Group leader	Tick when completed
Part 1		
Feedback on home practice Anxiety Education Compensating Also touch on: Special Play Thoughts, Feelings and Behaviour The Attention Rule		
Part 2		
Rules for giving effective praise Give it for *good* behaviour and for *brave* behaviour Sound positive when giving it Don't follow it with a criticism Use Specific Labelled Praise Give it as soon as possible after the behaviour Model acceptance of praise Focus on behaviours that you want *more* of, not *less* of		
Stairway to Bravery Teach parents to produce stairways for their children Get each parent to devise one stairway in session		
Home practice Practise praising good and confident behaviour Begin Stairway to Bravery Continue Special Play for around 10 minutes a day. Keep thinking about your TFB Keep thinking about your child's TFB Keep working on the compensating		
Key messages to be covered		
Using Specific Labelled Praise increases *good* behaviours and *confident* behaviours		
Parents need to model acceptance of praise		
It is not possible to praise a child too much		
Difficult behaviours, e.g. brave behaviours, need to broken down into little steps		
Key cognitions to be elicited and challenged		
If I praise my children all the time, they'll think they can get away with anything		
I can't praise my child when I am angry		
I do not want to praise my children all the time – the world's not like that. They need to get used to the big bad world		
My child should not have to be praised for being 'brave'		
My child should not have to be praised for behaving		

Praise and Encouragement

Using Praise to build confidence and self-esteem

Anxious kids often have quite a low opinion of themselves. This causes them problems when they meet a scary situation, as they will often think something like 'I'm useless, I can't cope with this'.

One way to build up their self-esteem is to use lots of praise.

There are two types of situations when you should think about using praise and rewards more:

1. When your child does something that they are quite good at. We all need to have things that we feel proud of, and anxious kids need it even more.

List here the things that your kid is quite good at:

2. Behaviours you would like to see more of.

List here things that your kid is scared of and could do with some encouragement on:

List here some good behaviours that you would like to see more of:

Using Praise

Praise is one of the most powerful forms of attention.

* Praise <u>all</u> behaviours you want to see more of, <u>every</u> time they occur.

* Try to be clear about what exactly your child did that you liked. This is called 'Specific Labelled Praise'. For example, "*Good boy for tidying up your room*" is much better than just "*That's great*".

* Praise should be used *as soon as possible* after the good behaviour.

* Make the praise sound like you mean it!

* Don't follow praise with a criticism. e.g. '*Well done for tidying your room, why can't you do that every day?*' This just leaves your child feeling fed up, and they are unlikely to tidy their room tomorrow!

Stairway to Bravery

We don't wait until our child is painting master-pieces before we give them encouragement. We give them encouragement for the blotchy, sticky things that they bring home from nursery.

Encouraging good behaviour, and encouraging brave behaviour is just the same. We have to encourage tiny steps in the right direction.

Name one brave behaviour you would like to see more of in your child

Some Examples of Specific Labelled Praise to Get You Started

* You are putting your toys away so well.

* Brilliant, you are doing just what I asked you to.

* I really like it when you share your toys with Sam.

* Well done for going into the shop on your own.

* Good boy/girl, you are sitting so quietly.

* Mum's very pleased with you for trying some carrots.

* Well done for going upstairs in the dark.

* Wow, what a wonderful job you've done of colouring that picture.

* Good boy/girl for making your bed when I asked you to.

* You're such a big boy/girl for stroking that dog.

* Thank you for letting me finish the washing up, now I'll read you a story.

* Well done for being brave and going to Amy's party.

* Dad is really proud of you for going to school today.

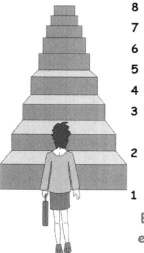

8
7
6
5
4
3
2
1

Break it down into easy learning steps for your child.

Break it down!

We don't wait until our child is painting masterpieces before we give them encouragement. We give them encouragement for the blotchy, sticky things that they bring home from nursery.

Encouraging good behaviour, and encouraging brave behaviour is just the same. We have to encourage tiny steps in the right direction.

Name *one brave behaviour* you would like to see more of in your child

---

✓

Break it down into easy learning steps for your child

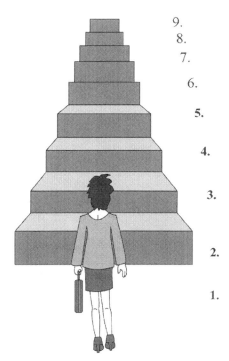

9.
8.
7.
6.
5.
4.
3.
2.
1.

Session Five

Using Rewards to Get Children Motivated

▶ Overview

In this session, after feedback on home practice, we talk about using rewards to motivate children to learn new behaviours. Anxious children's fear often impacts on their motivation to take steps to address their difficulties. So some external motivation normally needs to be provided to tip the motivational scales in favour of action. This session focuses on using small rewards in the most effective way to maximise their impact on children's motivation and behaviour. The session also details how to use star charts effectively.

▶ Before the Session

- Arrange room as described in Chapter Two.
- Laminate 'principles' from Session Four and stick them on the wall.
- Stick 'ground rules' from Session One on the wall.
- Stick up a large 'Seven Confident Thoughts' poster in a prominent location.
- Stick up the 'Anxiety Pyramid' poster.
- Collect a selection of blank star charts to give out to participants.

▶ The Session – Part 1

- **Welcome families**
- **Feedback on home practice**

Feedback will fill most of Part 1 of the session. It should follow the general guidance on feedback on home practice that is given in Chapter Two.

From Timid to Tiger: A Treatment Manual for Parenting the Anxious Child. By Dr Sam Cartwright-Hatton with Dr Ben Laskey, Dr Stewart Rust and Dr Deborah McNally
© 2010 John Wiley & Sons, Ltd.

Content of feedback

Feedback should be focused mostly on issues raised in Session Four, that is, praise and Stairway to Bravery. However, it is also important to keep referring back to Thoughts, Feelings and Behaviour (TFB), Special Play and The Attention Rule.

Praise

Key questions to ask:

- Has anyone done any Specific Labelled Praise?
- What did you say?
- What did you give it for (good behaviour or brave behaviour)?
- Did you remember the rules? Or, what did you do to ensure that your praise was particularly effective (e.g. give it asap; sound like you mean it; don't follow it with a criticism)?
- How did your child respond?
- What effect did it have on your child's behaviour?
- How did it make your child feel?
- How did it make you feel?

Stairway to Bravery

Key questions to ask:

- Who has designed a Stairway to Bravery?
  Try to run through everyone's personal stairway to check that
    o the steps are small enough;
    o the steps are in a sensible order;
    o appropriate rewards have been planned.
- Who has started their child on Stairway to Bravery?
- Did you get your child involved in designing it and planning the rewards?
- How did it go?
- How many steps did you try?
- How many times did you do each step?
- What reward did your child get?

Special Play

See Chapter Five for guidance on feedback on Special Play.

TFB, The Seven Confident Thoughts and The Attention Rule

Remember to also refer back to TFB, Seven Confident Thoughts and The Attention Rule as much as possible.

Troubleshooting feedback

The following are the most common difficulties that are raised in this feedback session.

- Parents have found it difficult to praise their child. An effort should be made to find out why this is so. Often this is because of a cognitive block on the part of the parent.

The main cognitive blocks to using praise were covered in Chapter Six. These negative beliefs and some suggestions for responding to them are reprinted here:

- ○ If I praise my children all the time, they'll think they can get away with anything.

  Parents often worry that if they praise their children too much, they will become spoilt or begin to depend on praise to do anything. We reassure parents that there is no such thing as too much of this type of praise. Children can become spoilt if they get plenty of praise but not enough limit setting, but praise in itself can do nothing but good.

- ○ I can't praise my child when I am angry.

  This is very honest. It is extremely difficult to praise a behaviour when you are very upset about other things that the child is doing. However, parents should be encouraged to use their skills of 'Botox Face' and 'Oscar-Winning Performance' to praise the behaviour and cover up their anger. It may be helpful to revisit The Attention Rule and to re-emphasise the use of praise to produce a higher frequency of the behaviours that parents want to see. It may be possible to refer to a principle to emphasise this specific point ('praising a behaviour made it happen more/again'). Remember, if the good behaviour gets praise, the child will divert more energy into the good behaviour, and will have less time and energy for the behaviours that you don't like. Help parents to reflect on the impact of *not* giving praise and attention for the desired behaviours. If you don't praise good and brave behaviour when you see it, you might not get the chance again. Encourage parents to plan how they might use TFB to overcome their feelings in such a scenario and provide their children with praise (even if it *is* through gritted teeth). 'what could you tell yourself/say/think to make sure that you *do* give your child praise if the same thing happens again this week?'

- ○ I do not want to praise my children all the time – the world's not like that. They need to get used to the big bad world.

  The homework review in this session should refer, frequently, to the Seven Confident Thoughts and how praise can be used directly to impact on these. If children are to become confident, successful adults, they *need* to believe that the world usually is a reasonably fair, safe place. The use of praise is central to the acquisition of these beliefs in this programme and is a foundation of the rest of the course. It may be necessary to challenge parents directly on this issue or on their own relationship with the 7CTs to tackle this potential barrier. Ask the parents whether it is possible for a child who believes in a big, bad world to ever be a truly confident person?

- ○ My child should not have to be praised for being 'brave' or my child should not have to be praised for behaving.

  Parents are often frustrated that their child cannot do things that may be normal for other children of the same age. If this frustration spills over, and they cannot praise their child for small steps towards their goals, then these goals are unlikely to be achieved. We talk to parents about how famous artists achieved their success? Did their parents wait until they were producing masterpieces before they praised them? Of course not; children need to be praised for the sticky, blotchy things that they bring home from nursery. This way, their confidence grows and only then can they take further steps towards success. This is the same for any new behaviour. Indeed, it's *particularly* important that parents praise behaviours that their children are struggling with.

- In addition, parents sometimes say that their children have not done anything that they could praise. In this case, it is helpful to reiterate that parents should be looking for tiny behaviours that are moving in the right direction, and should not wait for perfection before they praise. It can be very helpful to help the parents to identify some behaviours that they can set out to praise this week and to ask them to plan in detail how they will achieve this ('how will you spot what your child is doing . . . ?' 'when is that most likely to happen?', 'what will you say tohim/her?', 'what might stop you from praising him/her in that situation?'). The more detailed a plan the parent makes, the more likely it becomes that they will be successful in altering the child's behaviour.

- Parents can face a number of obstacles with Stairway to Bravery:
  - I couldn't get my child to try the first/second/nth step.
    In this case, you should consider whether the step was too hard for the child. Help the parents to think of an easier step to try. It is also possible that no reward was promised, or the reward was not sufficiently motivating for the child. Also consider whether the parents have been reliable about giving rewards in the past. The remainder of this session focuses on using rewards to maximum effect.
  - My child tried to do it but became so distressed that we had to give up.
    Congratulate the parents for giving it a go, and reassure them that no long-term damage has been done to their child. Examine in detail how they managed the situation. Ensure that the step was not too big, and that the child was not too tired to be attempting it. Encourage the parents to try again using a smaller step. Remember that group leaders should take the blame for failure while parents get the credit for success. It is often easy to claim that we did not explain in sufficient detail or missed a crucial section out if parents have really struggled with implementing a technique.

▶ The Session – Part 2

Using rewards

- We begin with a discussion about using rewards. The following areas are covered.
  - Who rewards their kids?
  - Who likes rewards for themselves – what about the stickers that we give out? What about being paid at the end of the week/month? Everyone likes being rewarded when they do something good.
  - What happens if you reward a behaviour? Give some examples for adults and ask the group how it would affect their motivation/behaviour. Yes, you get more of that behaviour in the future.
- The rules for using rewards.
  - These are very similar to the rules for praise.
    See if the group can remember the praise rules from last session. Another approach is to ask parents to review the rules in small groups and feed this back to the larger group. This helps group bonding and helps avoiding putting anyone 'on the spot'.
  - Give plenty of Specific Labelled Praise at the same time as the reward, so that the child knows exactly what behaviour earned the reward. Demonstrate this by giving out a reward (e.g. a sticker or a biscuit) with no praise/label and asking what behaviour was being rewarded.
  - Always give the reward *after* the behaviour, not before.
    If you give it before, the child will have little motivation to produce the desired behaviour. We usually illustrate this by giving one of the group a biscuit, and then saying 'right, you behave yourself for the rest of this afternoon!' We then ask the rest of the group 'OK, what are the odds of Sheila actually behaving herself now that she's pocketed the biscuit . . .?' Then, tell another parent that they can earn a biscuit by doing the same behaviour – this demonstrates clearly the difference in effectiveness of the two approaches. Although everyone recognises that Sheila was probably not going to cause too much trouble this afternoon, the point is taken.
  - Give the reward as *soon as possible* after the behaviour that you liked.
    Children have short memories, and the longer you leave the reward, the less they will link it with the good/brave behaviour.
  - Never, ever forget to give the reward.
    Children need to learn that when a reward is promised, it will be delivered. Otherwise, they will stop trying. Also, it is important that children learn that they can trust their parents' word.

- Never take a reward away.

  It is so tempting to remove a reward as punishment for some subsequent bad behaviour, but this should be avoided at all cost. What if your boss came in to work one day and said 'you did some good work last week, but you made some mistakes yesterday, so I've decided that you're not getting paid'. You'd be livid. What are the odds of you turning up to work again tomorrow? Very slim. If a child can't be completely sure that he/she will *get the reward* and *keep the reward*, he/she will not want to make the effort. Guidance on more suitable consequences for unwanted behaviour are given in Chapter Eleven.

  - It needs to be something that the child *wants*. Explore with parents that different children will find different things rewarding. This can be emphasised by thinking about what parents would find rewarding and contrasting with what their children might like (Panorama, glass of Chardonnay, sweets and so on.).

- Many parents are not used to giving rewards, and need some help in working out what to use. So, we spend a few minutes brainstorming good rewards as a group. We ask parents to write down a few rewards that they think would work for their child. There is space on the handout for them to do this.

  - Rewards can be cheap or free.

    Some of the best rewards are free – extra time playing with Mum; a game of football in the garden with Dad; staying up half an hour late to watch the match; choosing what to have for lunch.

  - Rewards should not be expensive.

    If rewards are expensive, there is a risk that the parent will not be able to deliver. Also, the child will find it difficult to get motivated for smaller rewards in the future. Pound shops are good sources of cheap but exciting rewards.

  - Rewards can be something that you were going to do anyway.

    'Because you tidied your toys up so nicely, I'm going to take us all on a special trip to the swings . . .'.

  - Choose a reward that the child will like – not what you like.

  - Go easy with food rewards.

    We tend not to recommend using sweets/crisps as rewards, as there is some evidence that using food as rewards might teach children to attach overly emotional consequences to food, which is not desirable. On the other hand, we wouldn't prohibit parents from using them completely – they can be useful in an emergency. We'd leave the final choice on this up to parents.

Using star charts to motivate children

Star charts are magic fairy dust. Yeah, yeah, we hear you saying (some of you, anyway). But they are . . . when done properly. Unfortunately, there are a lot of pitfalls in using star charts, and if you get them even a little bit wrong, they don't work. Here is our list of crimes against start charts.

- *Sad faces on star charts.*

  Star charts are meant to be a record of a child's *success* and *achievement*. The moment a mark signifying failure appears (a black mark, a cross, a sad face, etc.) it becomes a record of the child's failings. No wonder we hear so many stories of children tearing their star charts off the fridge. Help parents to reflect on how this will feel for children and how it will affect their motivation.

- *Taking stars off charts.*

  This is a bit like removing a reward once it has been earned, and should never be done, ever, under any circumstances, no matter how vile the child has been. If the child has earned the star, it is his/hers for keeps. See above regarding motivation. Role-play removing a star and a child weeping and ask the group if this is likely to help motivation. Star charts must not be mixed up in punishment or they will very quickly lose their effectiveness.

- *Unachievable goals.*

  Some children will work for the stars alone, but in general, the star chart will be more effective if the child is earning stars towards a slightly larger and more concrete reward. However, the reward needs to be chosen with care, using the rules above. One thing that can go wrong is asking the child to earn too many stars before he/she gets his/her reward. For instance, we worked with one family who had asked their child to earn 50 stars before she got her reward. Unsurprisingly, the star chart didn't work very well. We tweaked it so that the child only had to earn three stars to get her reward, and it worked a treat. For the first star chart, we suggest that the reward comes after a maximum of three stars (it may be two or even one if the child is very young or the behaviour is very occasional), although this can be moved up to five stars once the child is used to the system, and may be a little higher for older children. For star charts to succeed it is vital that children experience early success. Otherwise they will very quickly lose interest.

- *Setting time limits on star charts.*

  In general, you want the reward to come quite fast. However, it's a good idea to not set fixed time limits on star charts. We have seen star charts fail because the parents said 'Get five stars in the next five days, and then we will go ice-skating on Saturday.' See if anyone in your group can see the problem with this. The problem is that if the child doesn't get the star on Tuesday, he/she realises that he/she cannot get five by Saturday, so he/she gives up. So, we would advise the parent to say 'When you have got five stars, then we will go ice-skating'. That way, it doesn't matter if there are a couple of bad days; the child will still be motivated to keep going.

- *Putting days of the week on star charts.*

  This inadvertently ends up as a record of failure (see sad faces) because any gaps in the star chart remain as evidence of the child's poorer performance. The child will quickly lose interest. Also, this imposes a time limit on the star chart and therefore causes additional problems (see above). Parents may want to do this so that they can 'keep track of how well their child is doing'. It may help (if this is the case) to revisit the point of star charts – they are designed to motivate children, not to monitor their successes and failures. If parents really need to track this type of information we would suggest (quite clearly) that they do so in a way that their child is not aware of so as not to derail his/her efforts.

- *Making the first star too hard to get.*

  Children can be suspicious of new innovations that their parents bring home from this weird course that they are on. In order to get them into the idea that star charts are a good thing, parents need to make sure that the first star comes really fast, even if it means giving it to the children for a substantially less-than-perfect performance. This is even more important if the family has tried unsuccessful star charts in the past.

- *Star charts for not doing something.*

  Sometimes parents try to use star charts to get rid of a behaviour. For example, we've lost count of the number of star charts that we have seen for 'not fighting with your brother'. Such star charts are almost impossible to administer and will almost invariably fail. The problem is that it's really difficult to spot someone *not* doing something (how long do they need to not do it for it to count?). Also, even the most aggressive children will have times in the day when they are not fighting, and could rightfully claim a star. Instead, the parent should think about the behaviour that they *do* want to see. In this case, they could have a star chart for 'playing calmly with your brother'.

So, these are our list of crimes against star charts. Parents should now have a pretty good idea of how to do a decent star chart. If there is time, we might ask parents to identify principles of effective star chart use on the board at this point. We give out some ready-made star charts to get them going. A very basic copiable example can be found on the following page. However, star charts work best if they are planned jointly between the parent and the child, so we encourage families to start making their own charts as soon as possible. It is worth pointing out to parents that they don't need to go and buy stars for their charts – it's fine to just draw them on.

Annoyingly, schools and some of the so-called 'experts' on the television are often the worst offenders when it comes to crimes against star charts. It is worth reflecting on this with parents.

STAR CHART

This star chart belongs to: …………………………

I will get a star every time that I:……………………………

When I have got………stars, I will get a treat.

My treat will be………… ……………..

Troubleshooting rewards

Parents often have a number of concerns about using rewards, and it is worth finding out about these before you send them away to practice.

- *I should not have to reward my child to get him/her to be good or brave.* We use the same ideas to challenge these beliefs as presented in Chapter Six on using praise. In addition, we discuss whether we would all go to work if we didn't get paid . . . ? Give an example of when you have done a favour for a friend, and then they have asked you to do something for them? What did you do? Of course, most of the time, if the request was reasonable, you were only too pleased to help out your kindly friend, in return for the help that he/she has given you.
- *I can't afford lots of rewards.* Reiterate that the best rewards are social rewards – for example, doing something nice with Mum or Dad. It is worth reminding the group that rewards really should be cheap or free. A slightly more expensive reward (e.g. taking a friend to the cinema) should only be used for big achievements, such as finishing a star chart.
- *I've tried using rewards, but it doesn't work.* Yes, but have you tried using them following our rules? Parents have often tried promising rewards in return for good behaviour, but have a history of forgetting to give them, or setting the goalposts too high, or taking them away for subsequent bad behaviour. In these cases, parents will need to win the children's trust back by showing them that from now onwards, rewards really will be rewarding!

Home practice

- Practise using rewards for good behaviours.
- Practise using rewards for confident behaviours.
- Continue praising good and confident behaviour.
- Continue 'Stairway to Bravery'.
- Continue Special Play for 10 minutes per day.
- Keep thinking about your TFB.
- Carry on doing 'compensation', if needed.

Key messages for the session

- Rewards are a temporary measure leading to new behaviour.
- What reinforces one child won't necessarily reinforce another.
- Use realistic, inexpensive rewards.

▶ Key Cognitions to Elicit and Challenge

- I can't afford lots of rewards.
- I've tried rewards but they don't work.
- My child should not have to be rewarded for being 'brave'.
- My child should not have to be rewarded for behaving well.

▶ Don't Forget . . .

- Although this is a manualised intervention, remember the unique individuals in your group. Try to think about how they will each respond to the material in this session.
- Keep drawing out 'principles' and referring back to those generated by group members in previous sessions.
- Keep giving out those stickers to model reward and so that parents have a ready supply to use at home.
- Have fun! If you have fun, so will the group members.

Condensed session plan/treatment checklist

Item/concept	Group leader	Tick when completed
Part 1		
Feedback on home practice Praise Stairway to Bravery Also touch on: Special Play TFB and The Attention Rule		
Part 2		
Using rewards to motivate your child The rules Give the reward after the good behaviour Give the reward *asap* Don't forget to give the reward and never take them away Use plenty of Specific Labelled Praise (SLP)		
Brainstorm some good rewards Cheap or free Social rewards are best		
Star charts		
Home practice		
Practise using rewards for good behaviours Practise using rewards for confident behaviours Keep practising praise for good and confident behaviours Continue 'Stairway to Bravery' Continue Special Play for 10 minutes per day Keep thinking about your TFB Carry on doing 'compensation', if needed		
Key messages to be covered		
Rewards are a temporary measure leading to new behaviour		
What reinforces one child won't necessarily reinforce another		
Use realistic, inexpensive rewards		
Key cognitions to be elicited and challenged		
I can't afford lots of rewards		
I've tried rewards but they don't work		
My child should not have to be rewarded for being 'brave'		
My child should not have to be rewarded for behaving well		

This week Dr Esmeralda answers your questions about praise and reward

"Dear Dr Esmeralda,

My child should be able to go to the toilet completely on his own by his age. Should I really be praising him just because he can now go with me standing outside the door?"

Agatha Arkwright, West Wailing.

Dr Esmeralda replies:

Dear Agatha,

Going to the loo alone might seem easy to you, but to your child, it is as scary as jumping off a mountain. If your child has had to pluck up courage to do this, then you should definitely give him lots of attention for this. Praise and rewards are the best form of attention that you can give a child. If he gets specific labelled praise and reward for going to the loo with you just outside the door, perhaps next time he will feel more brave, and be able to tinkle with you a little bit further away.

"Dear Dr Esmeralda,

My child has been so naughty today. Honestly, sometimes I think I should have called him 'Damien'. I know I should praise and reward him when he is good, but today, when he tidied up the table after dinner, I was just too angry to reward him. What is a girl to do?"

Tabitha Titchmarsh, Gnashville..

Dr Esmeralda replies:

Dear Tabitha,

I know how you feel. They really can be little monkeys. But trust me, kids are smart, if he starts getting more attention for the good stuff, then he will switch his energies to being good. With a bit of luck, he will soon be putting so much effort into getting attention for being good, that he won't have any energy left for being naughty! And remember... TFB.

"Dear Dr Esmeralda,

I know I'm supposed to reward my little Drusilla when she has been brave. But I'm so worried! Won't she become dependent on rewards to get things done. And what on earth will happen when I'm not around to give a reward? Yours, in desperate search of an answer."

Herbert Hinchcliffe, Transylvania

Dr Esmeralda replies:

Herbert, be calmed! By rewarding Drusilla when she does something brave, you are being a wonderful parent. You don't have to keep rewarding a behaviour for ever. Once she has mastered a new brave behaviour, you can phase out the rewards. You can then start to give her rewards for a different or more difficult type of brave behaviour. Besides, children who get lots of praise and rewards when they are little, become very good at praising themselves. So, when they are grown up, they can give themselves a pat on the back if there is no one else around to do it. Keep up the good work Herbert!

Material in agony column reproduced by permission of Oneworld Publications

Dr Esmeralda's Agony Column +

"Dear Dr Esmeralda,

I've got a bone to pick with you! My 6 year old Mervyn is just so messy. I wanted him to be more tidy, so I decided to set up a reward scheme just like you said. I told him, if you make your bed, tidy your toys, clear the table, and put away all of the ironing every day, then I will give you a sticker. Well, Dr Esmeralda, I'm afraid that your fancy reward schemes don't work. He hasn't done one jot of tidying since. What do you say to that then?"

Timothy Turnpike

Tunbridge Wails

Dr Esmeralda Replies:

Dear Timothy,

Well, first of all, I would like to say well done for giving it a go. However, I think you might need to make some little adjustments to your reward scheme. Remember, when we are trying to encourage new behaviours, we have to encourage them little by little. By asking Mervyn to become an ace housekeeper overnight, I'm afraid you were expecting a little bit too much. Perhaps you could start by giving Mervyn a sticker if he has a go at making his bed. When he has cracked that, you can say 'Mervyn, you are so good at making your bed now, I think we should go to the next level of the game. Now you will get a sticker if you make your bed and tidy your toys up'. Also Timothy, I think you need to look at your expectations for your child. It is all well and good to get our children to aim high, but if we set them a target that is too high, we are setting them up for failure. If you are not sure what it is fair to ask of your child, maybe you could ask other parents that you trust, or you could ask Mervyn's teacher. Good luck with your new reward scheme".

Using Star Charts

Below are some tricks to help you use your star charts more effectively

Do's

Be clear about what you are giving stars for.

If you are hazy about the behaviour you want to see more of in your child, they are unlikely to be successful. Being specific about the behaviour you want to see will also make it easier for you to know when to give a star.

Choose small steps.

One reason that reward programmes sometimes fail is that parents make the expectations of their child too big. This makes the task seem impossible to the child and they will give up before they have even begun. By making the steps small, you can gradually help your child to make it to their goal.

Focus on positive behaviours.

It is important to focus on the behaviour you want to see more of in your child, and not on the behaviour you are trying to stop, e.g. reward your child for playing and sharing with their brother or sister, rather than for not fighting.

Get your child involved in setting up the reward system.

The ultimate goal of your star chart is to teach your child to take responsibility for their own behaviour. Getting them involved in the choice of rewards and the design of their star chart is great for getting them more motivated to earn the stars.

Cheap or free rewards work really well.

Rewards don't have to be expensive. How about a comic, something little from the pound shop, or extra privileges, such as staying up an hour late at bedtime?

Get the behaviour first, then give the reward.

Rewards should be given after the good or brave behaviours that you wanted to see.

Make sure the star is given as soon as possible.

It is a good idea to give the star as soon as you can after your child has done the good or brave behaviour. This keeps kids motivated.....and means that you don't forget to do it!

Make sure that you set an achievable target.....and make sure that the first star comes fast!

It is important that your child is able to achieve the target number of stars to gain their reward. It may be useful to leave dates and days off the chart so that there is no time limit in which your child has to achieve the goal.

Give a star every time.

For the stars and rewards to work, your child needs a star every time the behaviour happens. This way you can be consistent and you child will be clearer about the behaviours you want to see in them.

Keep it simple

If the reward system becomes too complicated, your child will be become unclear about what is expected of them. The simpler you can make it, the better!!

Don'ts X

- Don't make the goal too hard
- Don't mark up a negative on the chart
- Don't remove any stars
- Don't punish for failure
- Don't abandon the chart

Rewards in Summary

- Give rewards for behaviours that you want to see more of

- Give them for good behaviour

- Give them for brave behaviours

- Give the reward as soon as possible after the good or brave behaviour

- If you promise to give a reward later (e.g. "Because you went to school today, I will take you swimming on Saturday") you must stick to your promise even if the child is naughty later

- Make the reward the right size for the behaviour. Rewards don't need to be big!

- Give lots of specific labelled praise at the same time as you give the reward

- Always chose a reward because your child will like it, not because you will like it

- If you are going to give your child a treat anyway, tell them that it's because they did something good. (e.g. I was so proud of you going to the dentists, that I am going to take you to the park.")

In this space, write down some examples of rewards that you think your child may enjoy……

Session Six

Setting Limits on Anxious Children's Behaviour

▶ Overview

In this session, after feedback on home practice, we talk about setting limits on anxious children's behaviour. In our experience, many parents of anxious children find this very difficult. They have often found that their children become easily distressed when told to do something, particularly if raised voices or threats are used to enforce the command. Moreover, such children remain distressed for longer than the average child, and are difficult to console. As a result, many of the parents we see have stopped setting proper limits on their children's behaviour. The upshot of this is a highly stressed parent, who is then prone to overreacting unpredictably to a small digression, and a child who has very few boundaries. As we now know very well, all children, and *particularly* anxious children, need clear, reliably enforced boundaries, to feel safe, and to feel that they can cope and are in control. In other words, children need parents who can set clear limits in order to develop the Seven Confident Thoughts.

▶ Before the Session

- Arrange room as described in Chapter Two.
- Laminate 'principles' from Session Five and stick them on the wall.
- Stick 'ground rules' from Session One on the wall.
- Stick up a large 'Seven Confident Thoughts' poster in a prominent location.
- Stick up the 'Anxiety Pyramid' poster.

▶ The Session – Part 1

- **Welcome families**
- **Feedback on home practice**

Feedback will fill most of Part 1 of the session. Because there will be much to talk about in feedback (in particular, progress on Stairways to Bravery) and because the content for Part 2 of the session can be covered quite quickly, you should consider continuing feedback for an

From Timid to Tiger: A Treatment Manual for Parenting the Anxious Child. By Dr Sam Cartwright-Hatton with Dr Ben Laskey, Dr Stewart Rust and Dr Deborah McNally
© 2010 John Wiley & Sons, Ltd.

extra 15 minutes or so. Feedback should follow the general guidance on feedback on home practice that is given in Chapter Two.

Content of feedback

Feedback should be focused mostly on issues raised in Sessions Four and Five, that is, praise, reward and Stairway to Bravery. However, it is also important to keep referring back to Thoughts, Feelings and Behaviour (TFB), Special Play and The Attention Rule.

Praise

See Chapter Seven for guidance on feedback on praise.

Rewards

Key questions to ask:

- Who has used reward this week? What behaviour did you reward?
- What was the reward?
- What was the reward for?
- When did your child get the reward?
- What did you say to your child when you
    - promised the reward?
    - gave the reward?
- How did your child react?
- What happened to the behaviour that you rewarded?
- Did you notice anything else about your child? (e.g. was he/she more compliant, friendly or affectionate generally?)

Star charts

Key questions to ask:

- Who has tried a star chart?
- What behaviour was it for?
- What was the reward?
- How many stars did your child need to get the reward?
- How fast did he/she get the first star?
- How did your child respond to the star chart?
- Did you mark anything else on the chart – for example, sad faces, failures and so on?

Stairway to Bravery

Try to run through everyone's personal stairway to check that:

- the steps are small enough;
- the steps are in a sensible order;
- appropriate rewards have been planned.

See Chapter Seven for further guidance on feedback on Stairway to Bravery.

Special Play

See Chapter Five for guidance on feedback on Special Play.

TFB, The Seven Confident Thoughts and The Attention Rule

Remember to also refer back to TFB, Seven Confident Thoughts and The Attention Rule as much as possible.

Troubleshooting feedback

Much of the feedback should be spent on discussing progress on the Stairway to Bravery. Therefore, common difficulties with this, and some suggestions for dealing with them, are reprinted from Chapter Seven.

- Parents can face a number of obstacles with Stairway to Bravery.
  - *I couldn't get my child to try the first/second/nth step.*
    In this case, you should consider whether the step was too hard for the child. Help the parents to think of an easier step to try. It is also possible that no reward was promised, or the reward was not sufficiently motivating for the child. Also consider whether the parents have been reliable about giving rewards in the past.
  - *My child tried to do it but became so distressed that we had to give up.*
    Congratulate the parents for giving it a go, and reassure them that no long-term damage has been done to their child. Examine in detail how they managed the situation. Ensure that the step was not too big, and that the child was not too tired to be attempting it. Encourage the parents to try again using a smaller step. Remember that group leaders should take the blame for failure while parents get the credit for success. It is often easy to claim that we did not explain in sufficient detail or missed a crucial section out if parents have really struggled with implementing a technique.

- Some suggestions for dealing with difficulties using rewards are reprinted below (from Chapter Seven).
  - *I should not have to reward my child to get him/her to be good or brave.*
    We use the same ideas to challenge these beliefs as presented in Chapter Six on using praise. In addition, we discuss whether we would all go to work if we didn't get paid ...? Give an example of when you have received a favour from a friend, and then they have asked you to do something for them? What did you do? Of course, most of the time, if the request was reasonable, you were only too pleased to help out your kindly friend, in return for the help that they have given you.
  - *I can't afford lots of rewards.*
    Reiterate that the best rewards are social rewards – for example, doing something nice with Mum and Dad. It is worth reminding the group that rewards really should be cheap or free. A slightly more expensive reward (e.g. taking a friend to the cinema) should only be used for big achievements, such as finishing a star chart.
  - *I've tried using rewards, but it doesn't work.*
    Yes, but have you tried using them following our rules? Parents have often tried promising rewards in return for good behaviour, but have a history of forgetting to give them, or setting the goalposts too high, or taking them away for subsequent bad behaviour. In these cases, parents will need to win the child's trust back by showing him/her that from now onwards, rewards really will be rewarding!

Setting limits on an anxious child: introduction

We begin this section with reference to the Anxiety Pyramid. We point out to parents how much has been achieved so far. Now that the foundations of play, praise, reward and a basic understanding of child anxiety is in place, we can begin the work of managing those more difficult behaviours that anxious children often present with.

Setting limits: the importance of being clear, predictable and positive

There are many mistakes that even the best parents make when setting limits on their children's behaviour. We perform examples of these, and ask parents to spot the error.

- *Vague commands.*
  What is wrong with saying something like 'Pull your socks up! Behave! How many times do I have to tell you . . . ?' to a young child? That's right. Most of the time, he/she won't have the foggiest idea what we are on about. If you want a child to do something, then you have to tell him/her clearly, in simple, plain language, what behaviour you expect to see.

- *Failing to get the child's attention before giving the command.*
  We demonstrate this by pretending to yell upstairs 'Tidy up your toys please!' The problem with this is that the child might not have heard. Even if he/she did hear, you've got no idea whether he/she has done as you asked, and you won't know whether you need to follow-up the command or praise the child for carrying it out.

- *Long strings of commands.*
  'I want you to go upstairs, wash your face, brush your teeth, *don't* drop you towel on the floor, get into your pyjamas – the clean red ones in your bottom drawer, and don't forget to put your clothes in the laundry basket!' We give one parent this long string of orders, and then ask 'What was the third thing I said?' Very often they can't remember. So, we ask parents what is wrong with this command. Parents are usually quick to spot that it included too many orders for a young child, and that he/she is more than likely to get a bit of it wrong. This is bad news for all children, but is particularly stressful for anxious children, who are particularly susceptible to worrying about getting things wrong. For very young children, just one command at a time is ideal. As children get older, or a behaviour gets overlearned, slightly longer strings of two or possibly three commands can be used.

- *Tone of voice.*
  To demonstrate this frequent error, we give two examples of a command, for example, 'please tidy up your toys now'. First, we say it in a pleading, begging tone of voice. Second, we do it in a shouty, angry voice. We then Socratically elicit from parents the reasons that both of these approaches are problematic. First, giving a command in a pleading tone can convey the impression that the child has a choice about whether to comply or not, which, parents will agree, they do not. Also, it can give the impression that parent does not feel in charge of the situation. This is problematic for any parent – child relationship, but is particularly troublesome for an anxious child, who needs to be sure that his/her parent is confident, calm and on top of things. Second is the shouty voice. Clearly this is problematic, as it can be frightening for an anxious child, and does little to reinforce his/her beliefs that the world is a safe place, and that people are pretty nice really. Also, it can indicate to a child that he/she should use aggression when he/she wants someone to comply with him/her.

- *Questions, Questions . . . .*
  'Right, can you put your toys away now, please?' The problem with this is that the child is perfectly within their rights to say 'no'! We ask parents to think of another way of

saying this command, without giving the child the option of saying 'no', for example, 'Put your toys away now!'

- **Stop** *commands*.
  When parents want their child to stop doing something, they will usually say 'stop kicking the table!' This is a bit of a tricky one to explain but we sometimes explain it with reference to a fun bit of American research. This research used baseball players. The aim was to get them to hit the ball more slowly and accurately. So, the coaches would say to the players 'OK Chuck, don't put so much speed on the ball this time' (it helps if you can put on a bad American accent here). And what happened to the baseball players . . . ? Yes, that's right, they all ended hitting the ball even faster than before. The psychologists reckoned that this was because they had heard the word 'speed' and this had triggered their mind into thinking about hitting the ball fast. Their brains had then failed to process the word 'don't'. So, next time, the coaches asked the baseball players to 'hit the ball nice and slow this time!' What happened? Yep, they focused on the word 'slow' and hit the ball nice and slow that time. And children are just like baseball players. It is better to tell a child what to do, rather than to tell him/her what *not* to do. It is better to say 'please put your feet on the floor' than 'stop kicking the table'. Try a few examples with parents. For example, 'Stop arguing with your sister!' could become 'play nicely and share with your sister!' 'Stop shouting!' could become 'talk quietly please!'

In addition, there are a number of tricks that parents can use to increase the likelihood of compliance to a command.

- 'When – then' commands.
  When – then commands are like magic bullets. An example would be 'when you have done your homework, then you can watch television'. The child is told what behaviour is expected, and what small reward will immediately follow. The grammatical form of When – then commands is such that it is easily understandable by even quite young children, and those with mild language impairments. Practice some in the session. It is important to keep it positive and to ensure that the 'then' is always a reward, not a punishment. The parent should then follow the usual rules for giving the reward.

- Use the word 'now'.
  Parents sometimes feel a bit rude saying 'please set the table now'. But, if you don't say 'now', the child is free to decide what level of urgency should be attached to the behaviour. If parents want something done now, they should be encouraged to communicate this clearly to their child.

- Give choices and alternatives.
  None of us likes being told what to do, and children are no exception, but parents can soften the blow by giving choices or alternatives. For instance, saying 'do you want to wear the red socks or the blue?' makes it very clear to the child that he/she needs to put some socks on. However, importantly, it gives the child some *control* over the decision, and substantially increases the odds of him/her complying. Remember also, how important feeling in control is to anxious children. Similarly, 'you can't watch TV, but you can play with this game' is much more likely to get compliance than just telling the child to stop watching television.

- Remember your TFB.
  It is important to stay calm when giving commands. If the parent gets annoyed, the child is likely to get upset or dig his/her heels in.

- Remember to praise when the child complies.
  This is hugely important, but often needs lots of reminders. Once the child has complied, it is vitally important that the parent praises him/her for doing this. Ask parents to remember what using a little bit of Specific Labelled Praise does to a behaviour. That's right; it makes that behaviour much more likely in the future. It also makes the child feel as if he/she *chose* to behave appropriately, and, therefore, gives him/her a powerful sense of *control* over his/her environment, and reinforces his/her positive beliefs about himself/herself.

Home practice

- Practise setting limits as discussed in the session.
- Continue using praise and rewards for good and confident behaviours.
- Continue 'Stairway to Bravery'.
- Continue Special Play for 5–10 minutes per day.
- Keep thinking about your TFB.
- Carry on doing 'compensation', if needed.

Key messages for the session

- Household rules offer children safety and reduce misbehaviours.
- Normal, healthy children *will* test rules; don't take it personally.

▶ Key Cognitions to Elicit and Challenge

- It will upset my child if I order him/her about.
  Many of the families that we work with have had negative and unsuccessful experiences of trying to set limits on their children's behaviour. This has often caused extreme displays of distress that the parents have then found difficult to manage. In some families this is because limits have only been set once the parents are at the end of their tether, and have, therefore, overreacted somewhat. In others, it may be that parents place very few limits on children's behaviour or withdraw limits if children become upset, because they are fearful that their children may be damaged in some way by their distress. In backing away from setting limits on their children, the parents are not allowing the children to habituate to the stimulus. Therefore, the children do not learn to accept limits and calm themselves when limits are set. As we all know, anxious children need to face up to mild threats in order to learn to cope with them (remember the Dragon in the Mountain ...?).

  So, we reassure parents that with their armoury of new techniques, they will be able to set limits in a way that will minimise distress to their anxious children. We also explicitly discuss with parents how all children will predictably test limits set by parents to check whether the limit is a meaningful one. Behaviours that have led to the removal of boundaries in the past will often be repeated to test whether they have the same effect in the face of a new boundary. Parents need to be prepared for this testing and it may help them to consider how their children are likely to demonstrate this behaviour (the precise challenges will vary between different children). Also, parents need to understand that this testing does not mean that children do not want (or indeed can not tolerate) limits set on their behaviour; in fact the reverse is true. If the children do become upset, this is not because the parents have done something wrong. On the contrary, getting their children used to having limits set on their behaviour is a useful learning experience, and will help them to cope better with school, and with life in general.

▶ Don't Forget...

- Although this is a manualised intervention, remember the unique individuals in your group. Try to think about how they will each respond to the material in this session.
- Keep drawing out 'principles' and referring back to those generated by group members in previous sessions.
- Keep giving out those stickers to model reward and so that parents have a ready supply to use at home.
- Have fun! If you have fun, so will the group members.

Condensed session plan/treatment checklist

Item/concept	Group leader	Tick when completed
Part 1		
Feedback on home practice Praise Rewards and star charts Stairway to Bravery *Also touch on:* Special Play TFB and The Attention Rule		
Part 2		
Setting limits on an anxious child Common mistakes Tips		
Home practice		
Practise setting effective limits Practise using praise and rewards for good and confident behaviours Continue 'Stairway to Bravery' Continue Special Play for 10 minutes per day Keep thinking about your TFB Carry on doing 'compensation', if needed		
Key messages to be covered		
Household rules offer children safety and reduce misbehaviours		
Normal, healthy children *will* test rules; don't take it personally		
Key cognitions to be elicited and challenged		
It will upset my child if I order him/her about		

SETTING LIMITS FOR ANXIOUS CHILDREN

This week, Dr Esmeralda answers your questions on limit setting.

"Dear Dr Esmeralda,

I'm worried about this limit setting business that we keep hearing about. My friend Aspidestra has so many rules for her children it's just shocking. At last count, there were 1,312! And it does her children no good at all – it's like a madhouse, children running riot everywhere. I want my little Brenda to grow up in a world that feels free. I want her to see me as her friend, not her jailor. So, I have decided, there will be no rules in my house, and she can do as she pleases."

Boris Bunkoff,

Eyesore, Idaho

Dr Esmeralda replies:

Dear Boris,

I think you are right about Aspidestra. That is just far too many rules. How on earth does she manage to keep on top of them all? Rules only work if the parents can check they are being followed, and she must be exhausted trying to keep tabs on that lot. Now Boris, I am very pleased that you are putting so much effort into thinking about little Brenda's developing mind. However, I think you may have to make some little changes to how you will help her to grow such a healthy view. Did you know that children who have no rules do just as badly as children who have too many? Children who have no rules find the world very scary. They simply don't know what bad things might be lurking around the corner.

That is why us grown-ups are here. We set the rules to stop our little darlings from getting hurt – so that they can grow up feeling safe.

If we don't make any rules, how can we make sure our children are safe? How can we make sure that they do all the important growing up things, like getting enough sleep, eating healthily, and learning to be nice to other people?

I think you sound like a nice, sensible Dad Boris, and I'm sure you can think up just a few important rules that Brenda can stick to. If you just have a few rules like this, Brenda won't feel suffocated (she will secretly quite like it), and you won't feel like an ogre insisting that they are followed. Good luck Boris.

Dear Dr Esmeralda,

This Limit Setting is a load of rubbish. I've tried it all week with my Bernice, and she hasn't taken a blind bit of notice. Last night I gave her no less than five commands in a row, and she didn't do a one of them. It's a complete waste of time. Call yourself a psychologist?

Beryl Blewitt,

Upper Splatt, Norfolk

Dr Esmeralda replies:

Beryl Dear

I think you might be trying just a bit too hard! In giving five commands in a row you were just asking too much of poor Bernice. Children only have little memories, and they can only remember to do one thing at a time. Try just giving your little Darling one command, and see if she does a bit better with that. Don't give her another command until she has had a chance to do the first one. Hang in there Beryl, and remember... ...SLP

Dr Esmeralda's Agony Column +

Commands and Limit Setting

When you want your child to do something, you need to use a simple command.

How to give commands

* Decide exactly what you want your child to do
* Make sure you have your child's attention - eye contact if possible
* Give only one command at a time
* Tell your child exactly what you want them to do, for example,

   "It's bath-time soon, so please put your toys away now".

   "Put those bricks in the box"

   "We're going to cross the road, so hold my hand"

* Only give commands which you have time to enforce
* Just give one command at a time
* Use a firm voice, but don't shout
* Use "When...then" commands. It tells your child what's expected of them and also rewards them for doing what you asked them to, for example,

   "When you have put your toys away, then you can watch TV."

* Don't use questions. This gives your child the chance to say "No". So, for example, "Put your toys in the box" is better than, "Don't you think it's a good idea to put your toys away now?"

   Remember to praise your child as soon as they do as you ask

Keeping calm is very important, and very difficult!

You don't set a very good example if you have a tantrum yourself. And remember, you don't need to shout to show who is boss. 'Losing it' is called losing it for a good reason - the battle is lost if you get emotional because you can't plan and think straight. If you are feeling explosive, then go away and calm down before you return to tackle your child.

Don't start battles you can't win

Battles are easier to prevent than to stop. Avoid battles in public places. Try to distract the child first. In embarrassing situations where you can't win, it's better to give in right away than to give in after a fight. Save "No" for when you really mean it and stick to your guns when you decide to use it.

Give your child alternatives and choices

Sometimes you may want your child to not do something, for example, watch TV. It helps to provide your child with an alternative such as, "You can't watch TV now but you can play with this puzzle". When getting your child to do something they don't want to do, such as getting dressed, choices are helpful. For example, "Do you want to put on your red t-shirt or your green t-shirt?"

Setting household rules

To increase the chance of your child behaving as you want them to, they need to know what is expected of them. Setting rules within the house will make it easier for you to spot behaviours to praise and help you teach your child the consequences of behaving badly. For example, *Hitting your brothers and sisters is not allowed. You must wash your hands before dinner.*

Session Seven

Using Withdrawal of Attention to Manage Children's Behaviour

▶ Overview

In this session, after feedback on home practice, we return to The Attention Rule. As we know, children will do more of behaviours that attract parental attention. Helpfully, the reverse is also true; children will do less of any behaviours that consistently fail to get them parental attention. Therefore, in this session, we talk to parents about what behaviours can safely be ignored and then spend time teaching the ignoring technique carefully, using lots of demonstrations.

▶ Before the Session

- Arrange room as described in Chapter Two.
- Laminate 'principles' from Session Six and stick them on the wall.
- Stick 'ground rules' from Session One on the wall.
- Stick up a large 'Seven Confident Thoughts' poster in a prominent location.
- Stick up the 'Anxiety Pyramid' poster.

▶ The Session – Part 1

- **Welcome families**
- **Feedback on home practice**

Feedback should follow the general guidance on feedback on home practice that is given in Chapter Two.

Content of feedback

Feedback should be focused mostly on issues raised in Sessions Four and Six, that is, Stairway to Bravery and limit setting. However, it is also important to keep referring back to Thoughts, Feelings and Behaviour (TFB), praise and rewards, Special Play and The Attention Rule.

From Timid to Tiger: A Treatment Manual for Parenting the Anxious Child. By Dr Sam Cartwright-Hatton with Dr Ben Laskey, Dr Stewart Rust and Dr Deborah McNally
© 2010 John Wiley & Sons, Ltd.

Stairway to Bravery

See Chapter Seven for guidance on feedback on Stairway to Bravery.

Special Play

See Chapter Five for guidance on feedback on Special Play.

TFB, The Seven Confident Thoughts and The Attention Rule

Remember to also refer back to TFB, Seven Confident Thoughts and The Attention Rule as much as possible.

Limit setting

Questions to ask:

- Who has had a chance to use the commands that we talked about in the last session?
- What situation did you use them in?
- What did you say?
- What did your child do?
- What did you do next?
- How did that make you feel?
- How do you think your child felt? (link to Seven Confident Thoughts)
- Did anyone use a when – then command?
- Check that parents followed the key rules for good limit setting:
  - Clear, specific commands
  - Get the child's attention first
  - No long strings of commands
  - Clear, firm tone of voice
  - Don't phrase commands as questions
  - Avoid 'stop' commands
  - Use when – then commands
  - Give the child choices and alternatives
  - Praise the child immediately and enthusiastically when he/she complies.

Troubleshooting feedback

Some of the feedback time should be spent discussing the limit setting techniques that were taught in Session Six. The most common difficulty that arises with this is parents' reluctance to set limits on their children's behaviour. One approach to dealing with this is reprinted from Chapter Eight.

- It will upset my child if I order him/her about.
  Many of the families that we work with have had negative and unsuccessful experiences of trying to set limits on their children's behaviour. This has often caused extreme displays of distress that the parents have then found difficult to manage. In some families this is because limits have only been set once the parents are at the end of their tether, and have, therefore, overreacted somewhat. In others, it may be that parents place very few limits on children's behaviour or withdraw limits if children become upset, because they are fearful that their children may be damaged in some way by their distress. In backing away from setting limits on their children, the parents are not allowing the children to habituate to the stimulus. Therefore, the children do not learn to accept limits and calm themselves when limits are set. As we all know, anxious

children need to face up to mild threats in order to learn to cope with them (remember the Dragon in the Mountain ...?).

So, we reassure parents that with their armoury of new techniques, they will be able to set limits in a way that will minimise distress to their anxious children. We also explicitly discuss with parents how all children will predictably test limits set by parents to check whether the limit is a meaningful one. Behaviours that have led to the removal of boundaries in the past will often be repeated to test whether they have the same effect in the face of a new boundary. Parents need to be prepared for this testing and it may help them to consider how their children are likely to demonstrate this behaviour (the precise challenges will vary between different children). Also, parents need to understand that this testing does not mean that children do not want (or indeed can not tolerate) limits set on their behaviour; in fact the reverse is true. If the children do become upset, this is not because the parents have done something wrong. On the contrary, getting their children used to having limits set on their behaviour is a useful learning experience, and will help them to cope better with school, and with life in general.

▶ The Session – Part 2

Using withdrawal of attention (ignoring) to manage children's behaviour: what is ignoring?

We begin this session by revisiting 'The Attention Rule'.

Group leaders: *What do children want ...?*

Group: *Attention.*

Group leaders: *When do they want it ...?*

Group: *Now.*

Group leaders: *Whom do they want it from?*

Group: *Us!*

Having revised this concept, ask the group what happens when you give attention to a child's behaviour? Hopefully, someone will remember that the behaviour gets more frequent. If not, you can cue this by moving your arms upwards – this will usually trigger someone's memory. We then say to parents 'so, if paying attention to a behaviour makes that behaviour go up, what will happen to that behaviour if we take our attention away?' 'That's right; the behaviour starts to fall away'. So, although the fact that children want our attention all of the time can be very annoying, it can also be turned to our advantage; we can use removal of our attention – ignoring – to reduce behaviours that we want to get rid of.

Who has tried this? Does it work?

This is an important question to ask before you move on, because many parents will be sitting there, inwardly rolling their eyes. 'Just ignore it' is, we reckon, one of the commonest pieces of advice that parents struggling with their children's behaviour will have heard. It will have come from all sorts of sources, from Granny to the Health Visitor, but it is rare that this exhortation will have been backed up with any clear guidance on *how* and *when* to ignore behaviour. As a result, parents' valiant attempts to extinguish unwanted behaviours will have very often failed, and they are going to take a lot of convincing to give it another go; and fair enough. Your job now is to convince parents that ignoring is *really tricky* and it's not their fault if it's failed before. However, with your guidance and support, it *will* work, and will be the magic bullet that some of those tough behaviours need. To illustrate this point, we Launch into a couple of demonstrations.

Using ignoring

First, one of the group leaders invites a parent to come and practice with him/her. The parent is instructed to pretend that he/she is five years old and *really* wants a biscuit (but is not allowed to just go and get it by himself/herself). You, the group leader, play his/her parent. The parent (the five-year-old) is asked to start the demo by asking the parent (the group leader) for a biscuit. The role play then goes roughly like this:

Five-year-old:	*Mum, can I have a biscuit?*
Group leader:	*You can have one after your dinner.*
Five-year-old:	*But I want a biscuit now.*
Group leader:	*Well you can't have one. You won't eat your dinner.*
Five-year-old:	*Yes, I will Mum, I will, I promise.*
Group leader:	*No, you won't. That's what you said last night, and what happened? You didn't eat half your dinner*
Five-year-old:	*But Mum, I'm so hungryyyyyyy. I'm starving* (begins to whinge).
Group leader:	*I'm not listening. La la la.*
Five-year-old:	(Angry now) *I hate you.*
Group leader:	*Don't you speak to me like that. You wait until your father gets home.*
Five-year-old:	(Crying and throwing a tantrum) **But i want a biscuit**.
Group leader:	(Stops the exercise) *OK, Let's just pause it there.*
Group leader:	*Right, now I want to do the same thing, but I'm going to act slightly differently. Same again, I'm your parent, you really want a biscuit, but you can't just go and get it yourself. Start by asking me for a biscuit!*
Five-year-old:	*Mum, can I have a biscuit?*
Group leader:	*When you've had your dinner . . . Then you can have a biscuit.*
Five-year-old:	*But I want a biscuit now.*
Group leader:	Turns away from the child and mimes getting on with making dinner. Says nothing to the child.
Five-year-old:	*Muuuum, I want a biscuit.*
Group leader:	Continues facing away from child and gets on with dinner. Says nothing, does not look at or touch the child
Five-year-old:	*Muuuuuuuuuum! Can I have a biscuit. I'm* **starving** *Mum.*
Group leader:	Continues to ignore the child's nagging. Does not look at, speak to or touch the child. Moves away if necessary or distracts himself/herself with another activity (e.g. reading the paper, looking out of window, etc.).
Five-year-old:	Says nothing. The parent playing the child is looking a bit embarrassed or laughing by now.
Group leader:	(Ends the exercise). *Ok, well done. Let's have a round of applause and a sticker for Paula. Didn't she make a fantastic five-year-old?*

Draw out principles from the role plays

- Ask the parent who played the five-year-old which time she felt most likely to get the biscuit. Most people will agree that the first role play was most likely to end with the parent cracking and giving the child a biscuit.
- Ask the parents which demo was most likely to end with the parent and child in a huge argument. Most will agree it was the first.
- Ask the parents which demo was most likely to end with everyone having a calm and happy dinner. Most will agree it was the second.
- Ask the parents which demo was most stressful for the parent and which one was most stressful for the child. Most will agree it was the first.
- So, what were the main differences in the parent's behaviour in the second demo? Ask parents to shout these out.
  - The parent did not speak to the child *at all* after the initial when – then command.
  - The parent distracted herself, to keep herself calm, and also to give a strong message to the child that she was not engaging in this argument.
  - The parent did not look at the child. Removing eye contact is a very good way of cutting any conversation dead – it works with children as well as it does with adults. This also helps if the parent is feeling strong emotions (e.g. amusement or anger) as it is important that the child does not see this.
  - The parent did not touch the child at all.

What behaviours can be ignored?

Of course, ignoring won't work for all behaviours, and other behaviours would be dangerous to ignore. So, we work with parents to generate a list of what you can ignore and you can't.

- Behaviours that you can ignore.
  Most behaviours that are annoying but are *not* harmful or destructive – so, you can ignore moaning, whingeing, tantrums, swearing, nagging. It may be necessary to have quite protracted discussions around some behaviours that parents will feel worried about ignoring. Swearing is often particularly evocative of strong emotions and parents may say that they 'can't just ignore swearing'. Such reservations are normal and the group conversations that result from them are often essential for enhancing group learning about the techniques. The central points to draw out of such a discussion are as follows.
  Why do children in this age group swear? (They are normally copying something they have heard elsewhere, possibly from parents.) *What are they generally trying to get by using swear words?* (A reaction – attention – from parents.)
  How well do children understand the words they are using? (Normally, not at all. They use the words because of the response they generate.)
  What will happen if those words no longer gain the desired reaction (attention) from parents? (The behaviour will stop.)
  It may be helpful to include a role play to demonstrate this in the discussion at some point. Following such a conversation, we will normally leave parents to make up their own minds about how to proceed with respect to disputed behaviours. People who continue to doubt the efficacy of the technique will often be won round by their success with other behaviours or by the successes of other parents in the following week.
- Behaviours that you can't ignore.
  Anything that is dangerous. If the behaviour is posing a risk to the child or to anyone else, it can't be ignored.
  Anything that is damaging things. If the behaviour could cause a breakage, it usually can't be ignored. Parents may choose to ignore behaviours that put the child's own (inexpensive) things at risk.

Non-compliance. If a child refuses to comply with a parental command, this cannot be ignored. Ask your group if they can think why. This is because the child will learn that if they ignore your commands, they will be able to get away with not doing as they are told. Clearly, this is not a good thing in terms of parental control.

- Borderline behaviours.
  Headbanging, breath-holding and so on. We think that, in the vast majority of children with no disabilities, parents can safely ignore these behaviours, and would be well-advised to do so. However, we also think that this should be a decision for the parent to make. We discuss with parents what would happen to the breath-holding child if the behaviour were to be ignored. In the unlikely event that the child continued breath-holding until he/she began to suffocate, the body's self-preservation system would start up, and the child would begin breathing again. For headbanging, we ask the parents whether the child ever does this behaviour when there is no audience watching? In the majority of cases, the parents agree that it is a behaviour that is entirely driven by having an audience, and that by removing the attention that it gets, it will probably go away. We discuss the likely consequence of continuing to provide attention to the behaviour. Groups normally quickly identify that this will be likely to lead to a continuation of the behaviour. We also reassure parents that healthy children with no disabilities very rarely actually bang their heads hard enough to do any damage. Some parents with particular vulnerabilities may still feel unable to ignore certain behaviours (e.g. one mother who had a family history including a severe head injury felt that she would not be able to feel confident in taking this approach.)
  Worrying and reassurance seeking. This is a topic that we cover in much more detail in Chapter Ten (Session Eight). However, we like to sow the seed in parents' minds that *some* worrying and reassurance seeking is maintained by parents giving it lots of fuss and attention, and in these cases, after the initial worry has been dealt with appropriately, ignoring the behaviour is sometimes the right thing to do. However, we ask parents to wait until Session Eight before they begin to act on this information.

Tips for getting the most out of ignoring

- Behaviour will get worse before it gets better – this is often the principal reason why early attempts at this technique are unsuccessful: 'I'm ignoring it, just like they said and she's actually doing it MORE!'. Parents need to be fully prepared for this. You might choose to ask the group to predict the kinds of behaviours they are likely to be faced with when they begin ignoring. These include:
  - louder shouting/whining
  - anger and abuse
  - emotional blackmail ('I love you', 'Dad would let me have a biscuit if he was here', 'please, I'm so hungry …')
  - tears and distress.
  Discussion of these behaviours will go some way to diminishing parents' distress when they occur.
- No looking, touching or talking to the child when you are ignoring their behaviour.
  - If it helps, distract yourself from the child's behaviour, for example, by picking up a magazine or doing some tidying and so on. If necessary, and if it's safe to do so, leave the room, but make sure you can keep an eye on what is going on.
- Thoughts, Feelings, Behaviour Cycle: we take time to discuss the thoughts parents might have that will undermine their success with this technique (often linked to specific behaviours they will struggle to cope with). We then ask parents to generate 'alternative 'coping' thoughts. 'What can you tell yourself to help you to keep going if you feel as though you might be about to give in?' The list can be written up on the flipchart so that the whole group can consider coping statements that might help them. As part of this discussion we often discuss what would happen if we ignored a behaviour for a

period of time and then gave in. (The child learns that if they can go on for long enough then Mum/Dad will back down. They will, therefore, persist a bit longer the next time.)

- Ignoring only works properly if the rest of the Anxiety Pyramid is in place. It depends on the parent and child having a good relationship, and on the child knowing that switching to a more desirable behaviour will attract the parent's praise and attention.

- Once the child has stopped doing whatever you were ignoring, return your attention immediately and give them a bit of Specific Labelled Praise. For example, 'well done for calming yourself down'.

- Ask parents how effective they expect ignoring to be, the first time that they use it. For many children, the first try at ignoring will be fairly unpleasant for all concerned, and parents need to be aware of this. Talk about how the child will be unsure of the new rules, and will test them out by trying *even harder* to get the parent's attention. However, after the parent has stuck it out for the first time, the second time will be much easier, and the third time even easier still. Children learn quickly, but the first try can last a long time, particularly if you have a very stubborn child.

- So, where is the best place to try ignoring for the first time? In the supermarket? When you are tired and stressed, and at the mother-in-law's house? No, the best time to try this first is at home, when you have plenty of time, and when you are feeling most calm and in control.

Trying it out

We now cement these new ideas by inviting one parent to have a go at ignoring, using the new rules, of course. One of the group leaders stands in front of the parents. The group leader's job is to play a child who wants to watch TV, and to try to persuade her parent to let her do this. The chosen parent's job is to ignore this. The rest of the parents are there to provide support, encouragement and tips to the parent who is doing the ignoring. We would normally pick a parent who, we think, will find this very difficult to do at home for this demonstration – practising in the group will increase his/her confidence and chances of using the technique effectively at home.

So, the group leader says 'Dad, can I watch TV?' The chosen parent is instructed to say something like 'When you've done your homework … Then you can watch TV'. The second group leader is responsible for encouraging the other parents to shout tips and encouragement to the 'ignorer'. The second group leader should do this as Socratically as possible, for instance, by saying 'What could Mike do to distract himself? … Is it helpful for Mike to look at Ben, or not … ?'

Discussion

Ignoring is a tricky skill to learn and when used incorrectly, it can actually undermine progress. So, we finish with a brief discussion of a few important points.

- What happens if we ignore a child's nagging for a while, say 20 minutes, and then give in? That's right; we have taught the child that if they persist long enough, they will get what they want. We have trained the child to nag … To get round this problem, parents should learn to make a snap decision. If they are not feeling tough enough to ignore to the very end, they should give in *straight away*. If they don't give in straight away, they should stick it out until the child stops his/her behaviour.

- Ignoring is one of the hardest techniques to learn. And, sadly, it can be one of the slowest to reap rewards. Parents need to be aware of this. It is a tough skill to implement, but if you do, and you stick at it, it will be worthwhile in the end.

- How does all of this reinforce the Seven Confident Thoughts? This technique helps all of the 7CTs in one way or another. Particularly, it helps with 'I can cope with most things'.

This is because the parent is modelling staying really calm in the face of substantial provocation! Children will learn that they too can stay calm when all around them is chaos.

Home practice

- Practise ignoring unwanted behaviours.
- Continue using praise and rewards for good and confident behaviours.
- Continue 'Stairway to Bravery'.
- Continue Special Play for 10 minutes per day.
- Keep thinking about your TFB.
- Carry on doing 'compensation', if needed.
- Carry on the limit setting.

Key messages for the session

- Ignoring withdraws attention from children's unwanted behaviours, which is the thing they want most of all.
- Ignoring models staying calm in the face of a highly stressful stimulus.

▶ Parental Cognition to be Elicited and Challenged

- I can't ignore my child, it would seem so cruel.
  Many parents, particularly the more protective ones, are concerned that ignoring their child is abusive. We spend some time with these parents discussing the concepts underlying the technique (i.e. that increased attention causes behaviour to increase, and decreased attention causes them to fall). We then ask them to consider whether they are the sort of parents who already give their child lots of positive attention. Many of them, particularly if they have adhered to the earlier sessions, will readily agree that they do. We agree that a parent who always ignored their child would be classed as abusive. However, a parent who gives their child lots of attention and praise when he/she is behaving appropriately cannot be harming their child when they ignore an unwanted behaviour for a few minutes.

- My child will hate me.
  It is true that when parents first start ignoring their unwanted behaviours, most children get pretty cross. We discuss with parents whether this is likely to be a short-term or a long-term problem. Parents usually agree that their children's disgust will be fairly short lived, especially if they then get some rapid praise for the next desirable behaviour that they display. Also, in the long term, the parents are helping their children to control their emotions, and this can only be good for the children and for their relationship with their parents.

- I can't just ignore naughty behaviour, my child needs guidance on what is right and wrong.
  The key point here is that effective ignoring is an active technique, manipulating parental attention to provide children with *very* clear messages about which behaviours are acceptable and which ones are not. If a parent still has this reservation, at the end of the session, it may be helpful to encourage a group discussion – with examples of managing specific behaviour – to examine his/her beliefs. A doubting parent is more likely to be persuaded by other parents than by a group leader arguing with their point of view. Even parents who are unsure may be persuaded to try out ignoring on one specific behaviour for a week to see how it affects the frequency, duration and intensity.

▶ Don't Forget...

- Although this is a manualised intervention, remember the unique individuals in your group. Try to think about how they will each respond to the material in this session.
- Keep drawing out 'principles' and referring back to those generated by group members in previous sessions.
- Keep giving out those stickers to model reward and so that parents have a ready supply to use at home.
- Have fun! If you have fun, so will the group members.

Condensed session plan/treatment checklist

Item/concept	Group leader	Tick when completed
Part 1		
Feedback on home practice *Focus on*: Stairway to Bravery Limit setting *Also touch on*: Special Play Praise and rewards TFB and The Attention Rule		
Part 2		
What is ignoring? The Attention Rule Who has tried ignoring?		
Using ignoring Principles of ignoring (role plays) What can you ignore? Tips for ignoring effectively Trying it out Discussion		
Home practice		
Practise using ignoring Practise setting effective limits Practise using praise and rewards for good and confident behaviours Continue 'Stairway to Bravery' Continue Special Play for 10 minutes per day Keep thinking about your TFB Carry on doing 'compensation', if needed		
Key messages to be covered		
Ignoring withdraws attention from children's unwanted behaviours, which is the thing they want most of all		
Ignoring models staying calm in the face of a highly stressful stimulus		
Key cognitions to be elicited and challenged		
I can't ignore my child, it would seem so cruel		
My child will hate me		
I can't just ignore naughty behaviour; my child needs guidance on what is right and wrong		

IGNORING

This week Dr Esmeralda answers your questions about ignoring

"Dear Dr Esmeralda,

I've been hearing all about this new-fangled way of controlling unwanted behaviour in children - this so-called 'ignoring'. Well I think it's a disgrace! I'm not going to just stand by, while my children swear and curse and answer back. They will think they can get away with anything!"

Disgusted and Horrified

Derby.

Dr Esmeralda replies:

Dear Disgusted and Horrified,

You are right - we have to teach our children what behaviour is wrong, and I'm sure that your children know there are rules about not swearing and answering back. Now what you have to do is teach them that they cannot get what they want by swearing or answering back. And what do children want....? That's right - ATTENTION! So, we have to teach them that they get absolutely NO attention for this sort of behaviour. So, when they whinge and moan and answer back, the best thing to do is ignore them completely. They won't think they can get away with it - on the contrary, they will find the ignoring most irritating, and will soon give up their moaning! Also, by keeping calm when your children are nagging, you are providing a very positive example for them.

"Dear Dr Esmeralda,

I think this ignoring thing is a really good idea, but the problem is, I'm useless at it. I can ignore the nagging for about 5 minutes, but then it just gets to me and I explode at my kids. I'm so hopeless, what can I do?"

Cinderella Snotkopf

Stoke on Trent

Dr Esmeralda replies:

Dear Cinders,

Well first of all, you can stop telling yourself that you are hopeless! Think about your TFB - telling yourself that you are no good will just be getting you down, and that won't help at all. Ignoring is one of the hardest skills to learn, and I am impressed that you have been trying so hard. However, you are right - ignoring for a few minutes and then giving in can do more harm than good. It teaches our children that if they keep nagging and moaning for long enough, they will get what they want! So, I will let you into a little secret Cinderella - when I have to deal with a moaning child, I decide whether I am feeling strong enough to ignore until the bitter end. If I'm not feeling up to it, I give in straight away. If I decide to go with the ignoring, I stick it out until the child has stopped moaning. Hang in their Cinders!

Ignoring

Ignoring is probably the most difficult form of discipline to learn to use. It requires a great deal of self-control and good acting so that your child doesn't see that you are rattled.

Ignoring is not the same as doing nothing

It is a very effective way of showing your child what behaviours will *not* get your attention. We all need attention. Children need to learn the difference between good and bad ways of getting it.

Behaviours that can be managed by ignoring

Whining, whinging, nagging, and moaning can usually be dealt with by ignoring. It should not be used when there is a chance of harm to your child or to someone else, or of damage to things. In these situations a different discipline is appropriate.

How to use ignoring

* To ignore your child, you must *not look* at them, you must *not talk* to them and you must *not touch* them.

* Don't use any eye contact or other expression or other sign of disapproval. Turn your head away or turn your back to your child.

* Once you start ignoring, do not say anything to your child.

* Once you start ignoring, do not give any physical attention to your child. Leave the room if necessary.

* Do something distracting to help you to ignore, such as reading a magazine.

* Stop ignoring as soon as the inappropriate behaviour has stopped. Praise the next good thing that they do.

When you start using ignoring, your child won't know that you mean it and at first will try *even harder* to get your attention...PERSEVERE!

CHAPTER TEN

Session Eight

Managing Children's Worry

▶ Overview

In this session, after feedback from the previous session, we focus on managing children's worry. The aim is not to turn parents into expert cognitive therapists but to give them some simple tools to use when their children bring up worries. We focus on the techniques of problem solving and behavioural experiments and also call on skills taught earlier in the programme, such as Thoughts, Feelings and Behaviour (TFB), praise, reward, exposure, modelling and ignoring.

▶ Before the Session

- Arrange room as described in Chapter Two.
- Laminate principles from Session Seven and stick them on the wall.
- Stick 'ground rules' from Session One on the wall.
- Stick up a large 'Seven Confident Thoughts' poster in a prominent location.
- Stick up the 'Anxiety Pyramid' poster.
- Blow up balloons, attach 'worries' and put into the 'Big Bag O' Worries' (see below).

▶ The Session – Part 1

- **Welcome families**
- **Feedback on home practice**

Feedback should follow the general guidance on feedback on home practice that is given in Chapter Two.

Content of feedback

Feedback should be focused mostly on issues raised in Sessions Five and Seven, that is, Stairway to Bravery and ignoring. However, it is also important to keep referring back to praise and rewards, Special Play, TFB and The Attention Rule.

From Timid to Tiger: A Treatment Manual for Parenting the Anxious Child. By Dr Sam Cartwright-Hatton with Dr Ben Laskey, Dr Stewart Rust and Dr Deborah McNally
© 2010 John Wiley & Sons, Ltd.

Stairway to Bravery

See Chapter Seven for guidance on feedback on Stairway to Bravery.

Special Play

See Chapter Five for guidance on feedback on Special Play.

TFB, The Seven Confident Thoughts and The Attention Rule

Remember to also refer back to TFB, Seven Confident Thoughts and The Attention Rule as much as possible.

Ignoring

Questions to ask:

- Who has had a chance to try the ignoring technique that we talked about in last session?
- What situation did you use it in? (Check that parents are using ignoring safely.)
- What did you say?
- What did you do?
- Did you use your TFB?
- What did your child do?
- How long did you have to ignore for?
- What did you do next?
- How did that make you feel?
- How do you think your child felt?
- Check that parents followed the key rules for good limit ignoring:
  - No eye contact
  - No talking to the child, or any other form of communication, including gestures or facial expressions
  - No touching the child (unless absolutely necessary)
  - Kept going until the child calmed down
  - Praised the child immediately and enthusiastically when he/she calmed down.
- Points to reinforce
  - Keep it up!
  - When you first try ignoring, the behaviour nearly always gets worse before it gets better. Encourage parents who have had a tough time this week to keep trying. It will work soon.
- How does this help the Seven Confident Thoughts?

The key point here is that using the ignoring technique stops the argument from escalating, so it finishes sooner and everyone stays calmer (at least after the first few tries). So, it helps a lot with the Seven Confident Thoughts.

Troubleshooting feedback

Some of the feedback time should be spent discussing the ignoring technique that was taught in Session Seven. This can raise a number of issues for parents that can stop them using the technique properly. Suggestions for dealing with these are reprinted from Chapter Nine.

- I can't ignore my child, it would seem so cruel.

  Many parents, particularly the more protective ones, are concerned that ignoring their child is abusive. We spend some time with these parents discussing the concepts underlying the technique (i.e. that increased attention causes behaviour to increase, and decreased attention causes them to fall). We then ask them to consider whether they are the sort of parents who already give their children lots of positive attention. Many of them, particularly if they have adhered to the earlier sessions, will readily agree that they do. We agree that parents who always ignored their children would be classed as abusive. However, parents who give their children lots of attention and praise when they are behaving appropriately, cannot be harming their children when they ignore an unwanted behaviour for a few minutes.

- My child will hate me.

  It is true that when parents first start ignoring their unwanted behaviours, most children get pretty cross. We discuss with parents whether this is likely to be a short-term or long-term problem. Parents usually agree that their children's disgust will be fairly short-lived, especially if they then get some rapid praise for the next desirable behaviour that they display. Also, in the long term, the parents are helping their children to control their emotions, and this can only be good for the children and for their relationship with their parents.

- I can't just ignore naughty behaviour, my child needs guidance on what is right and wrong.

  The key point here is that effective ignoring is an active technique manipulating parental attention to provide children with *very* clear messages about which behaviours are acceptable and which ones are not. If a parent still has this reservation, at the end of the session, it may be helpful to encourage a group discussion – with examples of managing specific behaviour – to examine his/her beliefs. A doubting parent is more likely to be persuaded by other parents than by a group leader arguing with his/her point of view. Even parents who are unsure may be persuaded to try out ignoring on one specific behaviour for a week to see how it affects the frequency, duration and intensity.

▶ The Session – Part 2

Worry

Is worry normal?

We begin with a discussion about whether it is normal to worry. Many parents (and therapists) work on the assumption that all worry is bad, and should be eradicated. This myth is particularly prevalent where children are concerned. People often have a very rosy idea of childhood, filled with children who don't have a care in the world. Unfortunately, the research shows that this is simply not true. It is completely normal for even quite young children to worry about things. So, it would be foolhardy to try to stop a child worrying completely. The aim here is to produce children who can worry productively, and who have some control over their less useful worries.

When is worry good?

There are definitely times when worrying about something can be a good thing. How many of us would have ever passed any exams if we hadn't got a little bit worried about them? Discuss this with the group, and find out whether they think worrying can be a good thing. However, beware! Some people have some very over-inflated ideas of how useful worry can be. Beliefs such as 'You have to worry to be a nice person' and 'If my child didn't worry about something, and then it happened, it would be his/her fault' are surprisingly common.

We think that when parents hold beliefs such as these, they are likely to be transmitted to their child, and to cause the child to use worry to excess.

We aim to have parents thinking that worry is *normal*, and can *sometimes* be useful, when used properly, and in the right circumstances.

When is worry bad?

Actually, we don't think that worrying is usually going to cause a child much harm, but it feels miserable and can take up a lot of time. Ask parents what they think is bad about worry. People sometimes have quite catastrophic ideas about worry. Beliefs such as 'She drove herself mad with worrying' and 'He worried himself to death' are commonplace. If a parent holds catastrophic beliefs such as these, he/she is likely to panic when his/her child worries. This sends all the wrong messages to the child (and is likely to reinforce the child in his/her worrying) and needs to be addressed.

What can you do to help?

Listening skills – The first thing that any parent should do when the child comes to them with a *new* worry is listen to what the child is saying. Ideally, the parent would be using a simple cognitive technique called the 'downward arrow' which helps to find out the core worry that needs to be addressed. Some parents seem to do this naturally, but after much experimentation, we have come to the conclusion that it is fruitless to try to teach it to all parents. It just gets messy. So, instead, we just tell parents to:

- Listen to their child.
- Ask lots of questions about the worry.
- Be kind and sympathetic.
- Never criticise the child.

Is it a realistic or unrealistic worry?

What you do next depends on whether the child's worry is a *realistic* worry or an *unrealistic* worry. Now, this is rather an artificial distinction, which we have made up for the sake of practicality. You won't find it in any academic books on worry. However, we find it useful for getting parents to distinguish between worries that just need a bit of problem solving and those that need challenging, for example, with a behavioural experiment.

Realistic worries

Realistic worries are those that are a real life problem. It's not in the child's imagination. For example, if a child is poor at spelling and is worried that he/she may fail the spelling test on Friday, this is probably a realistic worry. Worries like this need problem solving. Problem solving is a basic clinical skill, and we are assuming, if you are reading this book, you know roughly what it is. So, we are not going to give a lot of detail here. The tricky bit is how to teach it to parents in 15 minutes. We achieve this by means of an example:

Lee is being called names by a girl at school. What should he do?

- This is clearly a 'realistic' worry. It is a problem that needs sorting out. We begin by encouraging the group to shout out all of the possible solutions to this problem, and writing them on the board.
- We then go through the solutions, one by one, getting parents to shout out the pros and cons of each, just as you would with a child.

- For solutions that seem like a good idea (e.g. talk to a teacher, walk away from this girl) we give lots of praise and reinforcement when the parents shout out pros. But, using a technique learnt in earlier sessions, when a parent gives a pro to a less desirable solution (e.g. hit the boy) we give this much less attention, and move on quickly. We do the same with cons. When group members shout out cons to a desirable solution, we don't pay them much attention, but when they give cons to a bad solution, we focus on this and give it lots of attention.

- Having completed the 'pros and cons' analysis, we ask parents if they noticed what we had done to steer their answers. We encourage them to think about how using their praise and attention encourages the child to focus on helpful solutions, and move away from unhelpful ones.

- We then ask the parents to select a solution. Usually, they will select a good one, such as 'tell the teacher' or 'walk away from the boy'. But, for a young child, it is not enough to just come up with a solution. The children will usually need a bit of help in planning exactly what they will do. Which teacher will they tell? When? What will they say? Sometimes it is useful to do a role play with the children. For instance, telling a child to 'just ignore' the bully is a bit like telling a parent to 'just ignore' a tantrum. It's not as simple as that! So, if the child has to do anything complicated or new as part of his/her solution, the parent should talk through the steps with him/her, and if possible, do some practice runs to make sure that the child knows exactly what he/she is doing.

Unrealistic worries

We count unrealistic worries as those that are unlikely to come true, or at least, not for a very long time. So, 'there are monsters under the bed' or 'I don't want Mum to die' are usually counted as unrealistic worries.

These can be some of the trickiest to deal with, and we would always encourage the parent to listen very carefully first, to give the child a chance to get the worry off his/her chest, and to try to find out what the child is really worried about. For instance, with 'I don't want Mum to die', this could be a simple misunderstanding about how dangerous Mum's job is, or what her high blood pressure really means and could be put right with some simple information. On the other hand, it could be much more complicated existential anxieties, which the parent cannot be expected to 'talk the child out of'. Our aim here is not to turn parents into cognitive therapists. Instead, we aim to give them some simple skills for dealing with simple worries. So, for more complicated worries, such as this, we encourage the parent to listen, and having established that this is not a simple problem-solving opportunity, or just in need of some basic information, or a simple behavioural experiment, they should distract the child onto something more productive and distracting. We emphasise, however, that the parents should always listen carefully first.

Assuming that the parents have decided that this is a simple but unrealistic worry that needs dealing with, how do they do this? This is where we teach parents to use 'behavioural experiments'. Behavioural experiments are a device from cognitive therapy that is used to test out whether a worry is true or not. They are similar to 'exposure' but are more targeted and specific, and are aimed at producing specific cognitive change. Again, the easiest way to explain the concept is with an example:

Alexa thinks that her teacher will shout if she gets her homework wrong.

The parent knows the teacher and knows that this is a very unlikely outcome. But how does she convince Alexa of this? At this point, it is useful to remind the group of the story of the dragon and the mountain (Chapter Five). Ask parents what the moral of the tale was. Of course, the moral of the tale was that when we are scared of something, we need to go up the mountain and find out whether it is really true.

So, in this case, Alexa needs to go 'up that mountain' and find out whether her worry is true or not. Ask the group how she could do this. Someone will usually suggest that she makes a deliberate mistake in her homework, and hands it in to see if the teacher shouts at her. This is a great idea, and is the foundation for a 'behavioural experiment'. To get the most out of a behavioural experiment, it should be set up as follows.

- Decide, with the child, how he/she can test the belief out.
- Plan how the child will test it out. Make sure that he/she knows what he/she needs to do at each step.
- Practise the steps if necessary.
- Test it out.
- Praise the child for 'going up the mountain'. Perhaps give a little reward.
- Talk to the child about what he/she has learnt from this experiment. For instance, he/she has learnt
  - that it's ok to make a mistake;
  - that his/her teacher won't shout at him/her for a mistake;
  - that sometimes his/her worries tell him/her fibs.

After the worry

It is important that children learn to deal with a worry and then *let it go*. Once a worry has been dealt with, or a plan has been made, there really is no benefit in dwelling on it any more. However, letting a worry go is a very difficult thing to do. A cognitive therapist, working with an older child might use cognitive techniques to help the child to manage any further intrusions. However, these techniques are complex and require considerable skill, and are, therefore, not appropriate for teaching to parents on this short course. Instead, we advise parents to use distraction to get their child focusing on something else. Parents should direct the child to an activity that is absorbing and fun.

Very often, shortly after the worry has been dealt with, thoughts of it will pop back up, and the child will bring it back to the parent. How should the parent respond? Most parents think that the *right* thing to do is to go through the problem again, reassuring the child that all is well. But, if the parent does this, what are they giving? That's right; they are giving more *attention* to the worry behaviour. They could also be giving the child the message that he/she *needs* extra reassurance, and that the worry *needs* working through again. Instead, we think, in the majority of circumstances, that the parent should give the child a calm, brief message, such as 'we've dealt with that worry, let's forget about it now until tomorrow', and then ignore (using skills from Chapter Nine) the child's attempts to get further reassurance. The parent can again try to distract the child onto a more productive and engaging activity. However, if the parent is going to use this approach, it is very important that he/she gives the child an opportunity to come back and discuss the worry at another time soon. This can be done on an ad hoc basis; for example, 'if you are still worried tomorrow after school, we can talk about it again then'. Or, for an older child who worries a lot, the parent and child can set aside a regular time for dealing with worries. We call this 'worry time'.

Worry time

When working with adolescents or adults, asking them to set aside a period each day in which to do their worrying can be very useful. It means that when a new worry crops up, the clients can think 'I don't need to worry about this now, I can do it later'. Often when their specified worry time comes, the heat has gone out of the problem, and it doesn't need much solving. Or, even if it is still a major problem, the clients are in a calmer, more prepared state and are better set for dealing with the worry. Most importantly, it gives the clients a new sense of control over their worry – many learn, for the first time in their lives, that they actually can stop worrying thoughts when they need to. We think that these are useful skills for children to learn, so, we decided to try this with parents and smaller children than it has been used with before, and have met with some success. It is *only* appropriate for children who experience excessively frequent worrying (perhaps with a diagnosis of generalised anxiety disorder) rather than a child who just has an occasional worry.

In order to do 'worry time', the parent and the child set aside a regular time that they agree to spend dealing with worries. It is usually best to do this daily. So, for instance, the parent and child set aside 15 minutes every day just after tea to deal with worries, the parent should make sure that they are always available at this time. However, if the child does not want to do the worry time sometimes, that is fine – as long as they don't suddenly remember a worry later on – if they do, it should wait until tomorrow's worry time.

During the worry time, the parent should:

- praise the child for managing to put aside their worries until now;
- listen to the child's worries;
- use problem solving and behavioural experiments to deal with the worries;
- after the worry time, the child should be distracted onto something fun and absorbing to take his/her mind off what he/she has just talked about;
- after worry time, the parent should avoid getting into any more discussion about worries until the next scheduled worry time. The exception is if a brand new worry comes up. In this case, it is always appropriate for the parent to ask if it can wait until worry time, and if not, to discuss it as soon as possible.

Practice: Big Bag O' Worries

This exercise allows parents to run through a series of common childhood worries and rehearse the steps that they would take in dealing with them.

One of the group leader enters, lugging a big bag (we just use a bin bag), looking sad. She is encouraged to empty her bag, so that everyone can help her with her burden. In the bag are six balloons, each with a worry attached. A parent picks a balloon, and the group decide how the worry should be managed. After each worry is dealt with, the balloon is popped. (The balloon popping is an important part of the exercise, as at least one parent/group leader always hates it, which allows for discussion of 'going up mountains', 'facing your fears', etc. and it allows rehearsal of the skills needed to get a reluctant child to engage in exposure.)

We use the following worries, but you could also make up some of your own. We have listed the steps that we think need to be taken to manage each worry.

- *No one will play with me at playtime.*
  We are treating this as a realistic worry (although in some circumstances, it could be an unrealistic one). Therefore, the parent needs to take the following steps:
  - ○ Listening
  - ○ Problem solving
  - ○ Distracting
  - ○ Setting a worry time to discuss it again if needed and then ignoring any reassurance seeking.
- *My teacher gave me a special red pencil, and warned me not to lose it. Now I've lost it and I will be in really big trouble.*
  This would usually be an unrealistic worry; unless the teacher is an ogre, the child is unlikely to get into huge trouble for losing a pencil. So, we would encourage the parent to take the following steps:
  - ○ Listening
  - ○ Behavioural experiment (the child confesses his/her crime to the teacher and waits to see if the teacher goes crazy)

- o Distracting
- o Setting a worry time (if needed) and then ignoring.

- *I want to join the school netball team, but I don't know what to do.*
  This is a realistic worry, in that the child really doesn't know how to go about joining the team. Therefore, we would advise the parent to take the following steps:

  - o Listening
  - o Problem solving (thinking about the steps needed to join the team)
  - o Distracting
  - o Setting a worry time (if needed) and then ignore.

- *I've got a big spelling test on Friday and I'm scared.*
  This could be a realistic worry if the child is genuinely poor at spelling and has a record of doing badly. In this case, he/she needs some help in problem solving a study plan. However, if the child is likely to do well and is worrying unnecessarily, then he/she may need a behavioural experiment. Sensitive listening, as a first step, will help to distinguish the two.

  - o Listening (work out whether it's realistic or unrealistic. Work out what the real fear is – humiliation, detention, being shouted at, etc).
  - o Problem solving (working out solutions to do well at the test)
    or
  - o Behavioural experiment (deliberately make a couple of mistakes on the test to see if the feared catastrophe comes true)
  - o Distracting
  - o Setting a worry time (if needed) and then ignoring.

- *Rambo the hamster might die.*
  We put this one in because it is a common worry, but one that is not readily managed using problem solving or behavioural experiments ('let's kill Rambo, and see if it really does make you sad . . .'). There is no right or wrong way for parents to deal with issues like this one. In many instances, the appropriate response depends on the family's personal belief system. We use this worry as an opportunity to reassure parents that fears about death are common and normal in this age group. We also like to reassure parents that it is OK to talk about death to children.
  Therefore, for this worry, we recommend the following approach:

  - o Listening
  - o Distracting
  - o Setting a worry time (if needed) and then ignoring.

- *If I tell Mum and Dad my worries, it will upset them.*
  In truth, this is not a worry that many children are likely to present to their parents, but we include it, as it is a worry that many children do hold. We use it to open up a discussion about how to make sure that children can bring their worries to you. The key points are as follows.

  - o Always listen the first time a worry appears.
  - o Never, ever criticise a child for worrying.
  - o Don't get upset about your child's worries. If you get upset, he/she will just feed on this. If you feel upset, think about Botox Face, Zipper Mouth and the Oscar-Winning Performance (see Chapter Five).

Troubleshooting

We find that the biggest problem in this session relates to behavioural experiments. In particular, parents are worried that behavioural experiments will go wrong and make the situation worse. For instance, in the example we use in this chapter, the child is asked to make a deliberate mistake in her homework, to see if she gets a bad reaction from her teacher. We are anticipating that the teacher's reaction will be fine, but parents will often ask 'what if it goes wrong?' We explain that although we should plan behavioural experiments carefully to try to reduce unexpected outcomes, they do happen sometimes, and actually, this is OK. Ask parents, 'what is the worst that could happen here?' They will generally agree that the worst outcome is that the teacher will be having a bad day, and will moan at their child, perhaps asking her to correct her mistakes. We discuss whether this is a catastrophic outcome for the child. Most agree that this is not an awful outcome, and, indeed, the child will have learnt that she can cope with being moaned at, and can cope with having to correct her mistakes.

Home practice

- Practise managing worries.
- Practise ignoring unwanted behaviours.
- Continue using praise and rewards for good and confident behaviours.
- Continue 'Stairway to Bravery'.
- Continue Special Play for 10 minutes per day.
- Keep thinking about your TFB.
- Carry on doing 'compensation', if needed.
- Carry on the limit setting.

Key messages for the session

- We all worry, even children, and this is ok.
- Key techniques for dealing with worry – listen, problem solve, test out worries.
- Afterwards, be careful not to give too much attention and reassurance for worrying.

▶ Parental Cognition to be Elicited and Challenged

- Isn't worry dangerous for my child?
  Worry is not dangerous. Almost all of us do it, and cope with it fine. The worst that worry can do to a child is make him/her fed up and miserable. Worrying, when done in a productive way (e.g. by using problem solving and behavioural experiments), can be quite helpful and actually make us less stressed. If parents are still concerned, remind them of the story of the Dinosaur and the Caveman (Chapter Five).
- My child should worry about things.
  As discussed above, lots of parents have excessive positive beliefs about worry, such as 'people who don't worry are not nice' and 'worrying helps my child to be prepared for things'. Whilst some positive beliefs, such as 'worrying helps my child think about the future' are fine in moderation, you need to beware of parents holding beliefs that might be encouraging excessive worry.

▶ Don't Forget . . .

- Although this is a manualised intervention, remember the unique individuals in your group. Try to think about how they will each respond to the material in this session.
- Keep drawing out 'principles' and referring back to those generated by group members in previous sessions.

- Keep giving out those stickers to model reward and so that parents have a ready supply to use at home.
- Have fun! If you have fun, so will the group members.

Condensed session plan/treatment checklist

Item/concept	Group leader	Tick when completed
Part 1		
Feedback on home practice Ignoring Stairway to Bravery Also touch on: Praise and rewards Special Play TFB and The Attention Rule		
Part 2		
Worry Is worry normal? When is worry good? When is worry bad?		
What you can do to help Listening skills Is it a realistic or unrealistic worry? Realistic worries Unrealistic worries After the worry Worry time		
Practice Big Bag O' Worries		
Home practice		
Practise managing worries Practise using ignoring Practise setting effective limits Practise using praise and rewards for good and confident behaviours Continue 'Stairway to Bravery' Continue Special Play for 10 minutes per day Keep thinking about your TFB Carry on doing 'compensation', if needed		
Key messages to be covered		
We all worry, even children, and this is ok		
Key techniques for dealing with worry – listen, problem solve, test out worries		
Afterwards, be careful not to give too much attention and reassurance for worrying		
Key cognitions to be elicited and challenged		
Isn't worry dangerous for my child?		
My child should worry about things		

Helping Children with WORRIES

Sometimes worries can feel overwhelming, but when you sit and look at them closely they are not so bad.

That is what worry solving is all about. It is about breaking problems down and working out what to do with them. Children who learn to worry solve have a useful skill to take them through life.

Problem Solving

Take a good look at the problem. Have a think about all the different ways you could deal with it.

Eg. Fred got called 'speccy four eyes' by Sarah today at school. What are the options for dealing with this?

* Go and thump Sarah
* Call Sarah a mean name
* Tell the teacher
* Ignore Sarah's silly behaviour, she just wants attention.

Think about what might happen if you try each of the options.

Eg. What will happen if Fred thumps Sarah? What will happen if he calls her a mean name? What will happen if he just ignores her?

Let your child decide what is the best option. Try not to tell them the right answer - it is much better if they decide themselves. However, you can help them come up with the right answer by pointing out problems with the bad options, and giving loads of praise when they decide on a good option.

Sometimes there aren't loads of options to choose from. Instead, the child just needs some help to break the problem into little steps.

E.g, Katie wants to join the school Judo club, but does not know how to do it. Her father helped

her to write a list of all the little steps she needed to do so that she could join:

* Ask Miss Jones who is in charge of Judo club
* Ask the teacher in charge if she can join
* Bring home the list of Judo kit and give it to Dad.

Testing out worries

Sometimes our worries get out of hand. Instead of real problems, we worry about things that won't really happen.

If you think your child is worrying about something that is not going to come true, get them to test out their worry.

How to do it

Eg. Jo is worried about getting her homework wrong.

☺ Find out EXACTLY what your child thinks is going to happen. In this case, Jo was worried that if she made a mistake that her teacher would be cross.

☺ Listen to why that would be so bad for your child. In this case, Jo was scared that the teacher would shout or even hit her.

☺ TEST OUT THE WORRY. In this case, Jo and her mum made a mistake in the homework, on purpose. Jo went to school the next day to see what would happen.

☺ Afterwards, have a nice chat about what happened. Did the worry come true? Did the teacher shout and hit? Did Jo cry and feel upset all day? Usually the answer is No, and your child has learnt an important lesson.

☺ Give your child heaps and heaps of praise for being brave and testing out their worry.

Remember, it is ok to ignore a worry after you have first dealt with it. Set a time to talk about it later, then don't give your child any more attention for worrying. Make sure to praise the first good or confident thing that they do after they have been worrying.

1

This week Dr Esmeralda answers your questions on worry

"Dear Dr Esmeralda,

My little Kermit is a terrible worrier. He worries about everything all the time. He'll make himself go mad with worrying. What can I do?

Kenneth Comberbatch

Great Collywobbles

Dr Esmeralda replies:

Dear Kenneth,

Fear not, for all this worrying may make Kermit sad, but it cannot make him go mad. Worrying is quite normal. Now, if you want to help Kermit to worry less, remember what I've said about listening to children's worries, about problem solving and about testing out worries. I'm sure if you do those things, you will help Kermit to worry less. And remember Kenneth, children copy their parent's behaviour...I wonder who he has learnt his worrying from...?

"Dear Dr Esmeralda,

I did what you said, and helped my Deirdre to test out her worries about going to parties. But Dr Esmeralda, I found it SO hard. When I was sending her through the door, she was crying and I felt so sorry for her that I had tears eyes too. I kept telling her to be careful, and be a brave girl, but it was all so horrible, and I really don't think it worked.

Doris Dishcloth

Drisley

Dr Esmeralda replies:

Dear Doris,

I think it's marvellous that you are pushing Deirdre to test out her worries. If you keep trying, it will work. But you are right, it is very hard for a caring Mum to do. It is very easy for us to get upset as much as our children. But Doris, your little Deirdre will copy your behaviour. If you show that you are upset, she will be upset too. If you tell her she must be brave, she will think that there really <u>must</u> be something to be scared of! My advice is calmly to send her off to the party with a smile and a wave, and a strict instruction to enjoy herself. Show her that you think it's all going to be fine. If you really don't think you can manage this, maybe you should get someone else to take her to the party. Hang in there Doris, she will thank you...

Dr Esmeralda's Agony Column +

Session Nine

Managing Really Difficult Behaviour: Time Out and Consequences

▶ **Overview**

In this session, after feedback from the previous session, we focus on managing those really stubborn difficult behaviours. We teach parents to use time out and consequences to their best effect with an anxious child.

▶ **Before the Session**

- Arrange room as described in Chapter Two.
- Laminate 'principles' from Session Eight and stick them on the wall.
- Stick 'ground rules' from Session One on the wall.
- Stick up a large 'Seven Confident Thoughts' poster in a prominent location.
- Stick up the 'Anxiety Pyramid' poster.

▶ **The Session – Part 1**

- **Welcome families**
- **Feedback on home practice**

Feedback should follow the general guidance on feedback on home practice that is given in Chapter Two.

Content of feedback

Feedback should be focused mostly on issues raised in Sessions Four and Eight, that is, Stairway to Bravery and managing worry. However, it is also important to keep referring back to praise and rewards, Special Play, Thoughts, Feelings and Behaviour (TFB) and The Attention Rule.

From Timid to Tiger: A Treatment Manual for Parenting the Anxious Child. By Dr Sam Cartwright-Hatton with Dr Ben Laskey, Dr Stewart Rust and Dr Deborah McNally
© 2010 John Wiley & Sons, Ltd.

Stairway to Bravery

See Chapter Seven for guidance on feedback on Stairway to Bravery.

Special Play

See Chapter Five for guidance on feedback on Special Play.

TFB, The Seven Confident Thoughts and The Attention Rule

Remember to also refer back to TFB, Seven Confident Thoughts and The Attention Rule as much as possible.

Managing worry

Questions to ask:

- Who has tried the techniques for managing worry that we talked about in last session?
- What situation did you use it in?
- What did you say?
- What did you do?
- Did anyone try a behavioural experiment?
- Did anyone try problem solving?
- What did your child do?
- Did you manage to distract your child afterwards?
- What did you do next?
- How did that make you feel?
- How do you think your child felt?
- How did this help the Seven Confident Thoughts?

Troubleshooting feedback

Some of the feedback time should be spent discussing the techniques for managing worry that were taught in Session Eight. This can raise a number of issues for parents who can stop them using the techniques properly. Suggestions for dealing with these are reprinted from Chapter Ten.

We find that the biggest problem relates to behavioural experiments. In particular, parents are worried that behavioural experiments will go wrong and make the situation worse. For instance, in the example we used in Chapter Ten, the child is asked to make a deliberate mistake in her homework to see if she gets a bad reaction from her teacher. We are anticipating that the teacher's reaction will be fine, but parents will often ask 'what if it goes wrong?' We explain that although we should plan behavioural experiments carefully to try to reduce unexpected outcomes, they do happen sometimes, and actually, this is OK. Ask parents, 'what is the worst that could happen here?' They will generally agree that the worst outcome is that the teacher will be having a bad day, and will moan at their child, perhaps asking her to correct her mistakes. We discuss whether this is a catastrophic outcome for the child. Most agree that this is not an awful outcome, and, indeed, the child will have learnt that she can cope with being moaned at, and can cope with having to correct her mistakes.

In addition, parents often hold the following beliefs that can interfere with using the techniques properly.

- *Isn't worry dangerous for my child?*
  Worry is not dangerous. Almost all of us do it, and cope with it fine. The worst that worry can do to a child is to make him/her fed up and miserable. Worrying, when done in

a productive way (e.g. by using problem solving and behavioural experiments), can be quite helpful and can actually make us less stressed. If parents are still concerned, remind them of the story of the Dinosaur and the Caveman (Chapter Five).

- *My child should worry about things.*
  As discussed in Chapter Ten, lots of parents have excessive positive beliefs about worry, such as 'people who don't worry are not nice' and 'worrying helps my child to be prepared for things'. Whilst some positive beliefs, such as 'worrying helps my child think about the future', are fine in moderation, you need to beware of parents holding beliefs that might be encouraging excessive worry.

▶ The Session – Part 2

In this session, we discuss how to manage more stubborn difficult behaviours – the sort that cannot simply be ignored because they are harmful or dangerous, or because the child is failing to comply with a parental command.

By this session, parents should be getting skilled at persuading children to engage in more of the good behaviours that they want to see, and we would always encourage parents to try hard with this before resorting to the techniques of consequences or time out that are discussed in this session. However, there are always going to be situations where this is not possible, or has been ineffective.

Consequences

If children fail to follow commands, what should the parents do? This is a good opportunity to discuss how to use 'consequences' for anxious children. We tend to use the word 'consequences' rather than the world 'punishment', as we want to keep away from the idea of punishment and retribution. The idea is to teach the children that sometimes we have to do things that we don't want to do, or we get an unpleasant consequence. Indeed, the more naturally the consequence can follow on from the behaviour, the better the children will learn.

So, we want to help parents to come up with consequences that are suitable for children in this age group. However, we begin by presenting a list of consequences that we have seen used in the past, but which were ineffective for one or more reasons. These are shown in Box 11.1. We ask parents to discuss why the consequences were ineffective.

Box 11.1. List of BAD consequences for use in Session Nine

We will cut our holiday short and go home now

- This is very difficult to follow through with.
- If you do follow it through, it is *far* too severe for the behaviour that it is a consequence for.
- It carries on punishing for far too long after the behaviour.
- It punishes the whole family for one person's misdemeanour.
- It is just plain cruel.
- It will create feelings of hostility and anger in the whole family.

You will go straight to bed now

- This threat is difficult to stick to, particularly if made several hours before bedtime.
- It sets the bedroom up as an emotional, unhappy place, when it should be a calm, restful one.

- For some children, if their bedroom is full of toys, TV and so on, it will not feel like their behaviour produced a negative consequence at all.
- If it is denying the child meals, then it is cruel and denying the child his/her basic rights.

Wait until your father gets home

- This sets poor old Dad up as the 'big bad wolf'.
- It gives the impression that Mum can't control the situation on her own.
- Mum will probably have forgotten by the time Dad gets home so the behaviour will have no real consequence.
- Even if Mum does remember, Dad might not be in the mood to deal calmly and rationally with the situation when he comes through the door.
- Dad ends up giving a consequence for a behaviour that he did not see and does not understand, and, therefore, cannot act fairly and proportionately.
- It holds the threat over the child all day, which could be emotionally cruel, particularly for an anxious child.

I will give your pet cat away

- This is unlikely to be followed through.
- If it is, it is very cruel.
- It lasts far too long as a consequence. Consequences should happen fast and then be forgotten about. This will not be forgotten and could disrupt the child's trust in the parents.
- However, it is possible that this is an appropriate consequence if it arises after the child has repeatedly failed to treat the cat appropriately.

You won't go on the school trip next week

- The parents are unlikely to be able to stick to this.
- If they do stick to this, it's really too far in the future. The children will probably have forgotten what behaviour earned this consequence by the time next week comes.
- It is potentially humiliating to the children. Consequences should not be humiliating. This is particularly important for anxious children.
- It potentially interferes with the children's education, which is never appropriate.

You came in late, so you are grounded for a fortnight

- The parents are unlikely to be able to stick to this.
- If the parents do stick to it, they are ensuring that the child does not get to practice getting in on time for another two weeks. This is a lot of wasted opportunities to learn a new behaviour.
- This is far too long for any consequence to go on. Consequences should be over quickly and then forgotten. Consequences that last two weeks will cause two weeks of anger, hostility and resentment, which is not good for any family.

You won't get any dinner

- This is denying the child his/her basic human right to adequate food, and is illegal. Similarly, any consequence that denies access, however briefly, to education or healthcare, is cruel and abusive and breaking the law.

The rules for consequences

Just like everything else in this programme, there are rules for getting the most out of consequences. Having discussed the list of 'bad consequences' in Box 11.1, ask the group to produce a list of rules to apply when doling out consequences. It should look something like this:

- *Consequences should be given out asap.*
  This is particularly important the younger the child is. The child *must* associate the consequence with the behaviour that you are trying to rid him/her of (e.g. failure to comply with a command), otherwise he/she will not learn from the consequence.

- *Consequences should be over quickly and then forgotten.*
  While a consequence is going on, it is normal for the child to be sulky and upset with his/her parents. While this is fine for a short while, it is potentially damaging if it goes on too long. It is not good for any child, but particularly for an anxious child, to have long periods of feeling miserable. Similarly, while the consequence is going on, things are likely to be fraught between the parent and child, and possibly the whole family. A calm, friendly family atmosphere, with open channels of communication is vital for children's mental health, and is particularly important for anxious children. Therefore, it is important that consequences are over quickly, and are then *completely* forgotten about by everyone.

- *Consequences should fit the behaviour and should never be cruel.*
  If possible, the consequence should arise naturally from the behaviour. For instance, if a child refuses to put his/her bicycle away, he/she could be told that he/she can't use the bike for the rest of the weekend. Similarly, if a child won't at least try all of the food on his/her plate at dinner, he/she won't get anything else instead.

- *Consequences must never take away a child's basic rights.*
  Parents should understand that it is wrong to deny a child food, or access to healthcare or access to school. For instance, it is never appropriate to keep a child away from school for a day as a punishment.

- *The consequence is for the child's good, not the parent's.*
  Many parents find that giving out a harsh consequence makes them feel better – and assuages some of the anger that they feel towards the child. However, it is worth discussing what effect this will have in the long term. Although this makes the parents feel better, does it improve the child's behaviour? In fact, it does not, as the child then also feels hostile towards the parent, and is less, not more likely to comply with commands and requests in future.

- *Make sure the consequence really is a consequence.*
  All children are different, and just as they respond to different rewards, they also respond to different punishments. It is no use denying a child pudding if he/she hasn't got a sweet tooth. Similarly, sending him/her to his/her room may not work as a consequence if it is full of lovely toys and interesting things to do. Encourage parents to think about what will work for their individual child.

- *Consequences should not be humiliating.*
  Consequences should encourage the child to think about their behaviour, and work out how to do better next time. This will be more difficult if he/she is feeling very humiliated or angry. So, for instance, a consequence that shows him/her up in front

of his/her friends is likely to be ineffective. If it is necessary to dole out a consequence when there are lots of other people around, the parent should try to get the child alone in a quiet place to do it, and to ensure that the consequence can be completed without great embarrassment.

- *Consequences should give the child the chance to learn the correct behaviour.*
  We have all seen parents give out consequences that don't allow the child to learn to behave more appropriately. For instance, a child is drawing on a piece of paper, but goes over the edges and draws on the table. So, the parent takes the paper away and says 'you have drawn on the table, so no more drawing today'. On the face of it, this is an ok consequence. However, it will be 24 hours before the child gets to practice drawing neatly on the paper. This is a long time, and it's possible the child will have even forgotten the rule and the consequence by then. See if your group can come up with a tweak that will improve this consequence. We suggest that when the child draws on the table, the parent says 'you have drawn on the table, so no more drawing for five minutes'. After five minutes, the child gets to draw again, and gets to practice doing it right. The parent should, of course, remember to give heaps of praise when the child does get it right. Similarly, in our 'grounding' example, if the child is grounded for two weeks, it is two whole weeks before he/she gets to work on improving his/her poor time-management skills again. Can your group think of a tweak to this consequence? We suggest that the child is grounded for one night, and the following night, he/she gets to practice coming in on time again.

- *Giving in straight away.*
  Sometimes a battle of wills with a child begins. Let's face it; it happens quite a lot, even with the easiest going of children. However, for many of the families that we see, the parents will give a command, and when the children fail to comply, or moan about it, they will give it repeatedly and then eventually give up. Ask your group what the children will have learnt from this? The children will have learnt that if they just ignore the parents long enough, or moan long enough, the parents will give in. So, we say to parents that sometimes we all give a command and then realise that we haven't got the time or the energy to enforce it. This is normal. The best thing to do is give in *straight away*. This way, although not the ideal outcome for the parents, the children have not been trained to dig their heels in to get what they want.

- *Backing down later.*
  Sometimes children, for a variety of altruistic and not-so altruistic reasons, will work very hard to make up for their bad behaviour. For instance, one teenager had not come home in time to go to the dentist, as instructed by his parents, so they agreed that he could not watch the big football match on TV that evening. He was very upset about this, and made huge efforts to make amends. He did all the washing up, tidied and dusted, even did some vacuuming, and was generally a delightful, model child all afternoon. The parents asked us whether it would be OK to let him watch the match. What does your group think? We told the parents that they should still enforce the consequence. If they had allowed him to watch the match, what would he have learnt? He would have learnt that it is OK to do as you like – you can always win your parents round later. We advised his parents to give him lots of praise and a separate small reward for all of his efforts around the house, but that the original consequence should remain.

- *Changing your mind.*
  Sometimes parents give out a consequence, and then realise that they have done the wrong thing. In the heat of the moment, it is not unusual to overreact. So, although we think that parents should stick to what they say most of the time, we agree that, very occasionally, it is OK to change your mind about a consequence. If it is necessary to do this, the parents should explain to the child that in the heat of the moment, they overreacted, and that they would like to make the consequence less harsh. However, parents should be careful that this is not done in response to the child's moaning; otherwise there is a risk that they will be reinforcing the moaning behaviour.

Personalised consequences

There is space on this week's handout for parents to write down some consequences that will work well for their child.

Time out

Time out is also great for behaviours that you can't ignore, such as dangerous or destructive behaviours, or for non-compliance. However, time out should be used sparingly, so using praise and reward and consequences should be attempted first.

Time out works a bit like ignoring. In fact it is like 'super-ignoring'.

How to do time out

- Ask parents to choose a good place in their house for time out. This should be:
  - a boring place;
  - a safe place;
  - not a scary place and not their bedroom;
  - somewhere that they can keep an eye on the child without giving too much attention;
  - good places include the bottom of the stairs or in the hallway.
- Explaining time out to the children
  - Discuss with your group what the children need to know in advance. This will depend on the age of the children. However, at a minimum, the children should know that there is this new thing called 'time out' that will be used sometimes. They should know that the point of time out is to help them calm down. They should know that the parents will take them to a quiet place, and they will have to stay there until they are calm and their parents say that they can come out.
  - Parents should try to explain this to the children before the first time that they use it.
- The rules for time out
  - Time out should last for one minute for each year of the child's life, up to a maximum of five minutes. So, for a three-year-old, it would be three minutes, for a four-year old it would be four minutes, for a five-year-old it would be five minutes and for six years and older also, it would be five minutes.
  - However, the child also needs to stay in time out until he/she has been calm for two minutes. This can mean that time out lasts quite a while the first few times that you try it.
  - If the child leaves time out, the parent should calmly return him/her until he/she stays where he/she is put.
  - Just like during ignoring, during time out the parents should not give the child any attention at all, unless they have to.
  - There should be no touching (unless returning a child who has walked out of time out).
  - There should be no speaking (even if returning a child who has walked out of time out). The only time that the parents should speak is when they first tell the child that they are going to time out.
- After time out
  - The parents should find something to praise asap, even if this is just praising the child for calming down.
  - The misdemeanour should be forgotten about.
  - Sometimes children refuse to leave time out. This is fine. The parents should just leave them there until they come out of their own accord.
  - If the child repeats the unwanted behaviour, the parents should repeat the time out.

- Practising time out
  - The group leader should pretend to be a parent doing time out, with a parent playing the role of a child. Show what happens when a child leaves time out. Demonstrate calmly and silently returning the child to time out.
  - Choose a parent to have a go at being a parent using time out. The group leader plays a very reluctant child who shouts, moans, cries and complains to the parent. The 'child' should try to leave time out. The rest of the group are to shout out suggestions (e.g. 'don't say anything, just ignore him', 'just take him firmly by the arm back to the chair', 'don't look at him') and encouragement to the parent doing the role play. At the end, the group leader should refuse to come out of time out, so that the group can rehearse what should be done in that situation (i.e. they should just leave him there).
- Time out and the anxious child
  There are a couple of extra points to take into account when using time out with an anxious child.
  - Time out is not meant to be frightening, it is just meant to be boring. Make sure that the child is not frightened during time out. So, for instance, if a child is afraid of the dark, the place for time out should be well lit. If the child is separation anxious, the parent should stay close by.
  - Time out can be used by children who want to get out of doing something scary. So, for example, one child that we worked with would try to get put in to time out (and then throw tantrums for long periods) to get out of going out to parties, or doing other things that he was scared of.

Smacking versus time out and consequences

At the end of the session, we have a discussion about the pros and cons of using smacking (or other physical punishment) versus the techniques that we have discussed today for managing tricky behaviours.

We usually do this by writing the pros and cons of each on the board.

- Ask parents to shout out the pros and cons of smacking.
  - *Pros*
    - It's quick.
    - It's easy.
    - It doesn't take any thinking about.
    - It instantly makes the parent feel better.
  - *Cons*
    - It teaches children to be aggressive.
    - It doesn't 'match' the crime, in most cases.
    - It is potentially illegal.
    - It is frightening and can harm the Seven Confident Thoughts (ask your group which ones).
    - The child can stay angry and resentful for a long time afterwards.
- Discuss the pros and cons of time out and consequences
  - *Pros*
    - Time out teaches the child how to calm themselves down.
    - The parent is likely to be calmer at the end too.
    - They don't usually take too long (after the first few tries).
    - They model the parent staying calm in the face of stress.
  - *Cons*
    - Time out can take a long time the first few times that you do it. However, if you stick with it, the child learns that if he/she calms down quickly, he/she will be out quickly.
    - They are more difficult to do when you are away from home, but not impossible, with a little creative thought.

At the end of this exercise, ask parents which approach they think is better. Hopefully, and in our experience, most parents by this stage of the course have decided that smacking is not a useful approach to behaviour management.

Home practice

- Practise using time out and consequences, as necessary.
- Practise managing worries.
- Practise ignoring unwanted behaviours.
- Continue using praise and rewards for good and confident behaviours.
- Continue 'Stairway to Bravery'.
- Continue Special Play for 10 minutes per day.
- Keep thinking about your TFB.
- Carry on doing 'compensation', if needed.
- Carry on the limit setting.

Key messages for the session

- Consequences and time out are great for managing non-compliance and for dangerous and destructive behaviours.
- Consequences and time out should only be used when praise and rewards have failed to work alone.
- Time out should be used sparingly.
- Time out and consequences are safer and more effective than physical punishments.

▶ Parental Cognition to be Elicited and Challenged

- I am scared to punish my child – he/she gets so upset.
  Many of the families that we see have been trained by their children so as not to impose any limits on their behaviour. They very often have children who become distressed easily, and are then difficult to console. So, for the sake of a quiet family life, and to protect their children from distress, the parents have stopped setting limits. However, if this is the case for any of your families, you should get them to consider the effects that this will have on the Seven Confident Thoughts. In general, families that have a clear set of rules and a clear, reliable set of consequences for breaking them have more confident children, who know that the world is a safe place, and who feel in control of what happens to them. Without these boundaries, children never know what is round the corner. We find that although a lot of the parents whom we see are quite lax in their rule enforcement, this makes family life very stressful, and these parents are more prone to snapping and imposing harsh and unfair punishments that really do cause their children genuine upset. In summary, a few rules, fairly and consistently applied are good for anxious children, and parents should not feel afraid to use them. In the case of very anxious parents, they may need to be encouraged to take very small steps towards using consequences and time out for the first time.

▶ Don't Forget . . .

- Although this is a manualised intervention, remember the unique individuals in your group. Try to think about how they will each respond to the material in this session.
- Keep drawing out 'principles' and referring back to those generated by group members in previous sessions.

- Keep giving out those stickers to model reward and so that parents have a ready supply to use at home.
- Have fun! If you have fun, so will the group members.

Condensed session plan/treatment checklist

Item/concept	Group leader	Tick when completed
Part 1		
Feedback on home practice		
Focus on:		
Managing worry		
Stairway to Bravery		
Also touch on:		
Praise and rewards		
Special Play		
TFB and The Attention Rule		
Part 2		
Consequences		
What is an acceptable consequence?		
The rules for consequences		
Personalised consequences		
How to do time out		
Choosing a place		
Explaining time out to the child		
The rules for time out		
After time out		
Practising time out		
Time out and the anxious child		
Smacking versus time out and consequences		
Home practice		
Practise using time out and consequences as necessary		
Practise managing worries		
Practise using ignoring		
Practise setting effective limits		
Practise using praise and rewards for good and confident behaviours		
Continue 'Stairway to Bravery'		
Continue Special Play for 10 minutes per day		
Keep thinking about your TFB		
Carry on doing 'compensation', if needed		
Key messages to be covered		
Consequences and time out are great for managing non-compliance and for dangerous and destructive behaviours		
Consequences and time out should only be used when praise and rewards have failed to work alone		
Time out should be used sparingly		
Time out and consequences are safer and more effective than physical punishments		
Key cognitions to be elicited and challenged		
I am scared to punish my child – they get so upset		

TIME OUT & CONSEQUENCES

This week, Dr Esmeralda answers your questions on time out and consequences

Dear Dr Esmeralda,

I like this Time Out business, it has really helped my little Semolina to stop biting. For some reason though, it won't work at all with my son. Little Simeon is scared of dogs, and we have been doing Learning Steps to get him used to them. The next step is to stroke next door's dog. However, every time I tell him to do it, he refuses. I have sent him to Time Out 10 times now, for refusing to do it, and still he won't go near little fluffy!"

Arabella Splatt
Leighton Buzzoff

Dr Esmeralda replies:

Dear Arabella,

I am so glad that you are trying Learning Steps to get Simeon used to dogs. It really does work. But Simeon has clearly got stuck. I wonder if you need to have another think about your stairway to bravery. Perhaps the latest step is just too big! Even us psychologists get it wrong sometimes you know! Try making the step smaller – maybe he just has to go in the same room as Fluffy to start with.

Also, have you tried using rewards to get Simeon to do his Learning Steps? Rewards should always be tried before you resort to Time Out. Good luck Arabella, and don't give up!

Dear Dr Esmeralda,

I've tried and tried with this Time Out, but it's not working, and I'm absolutely exhausted. I started by giving Time Out for 5 minutes, like you said, but that didn't work – she said she LIKED being in Time Out. So, I started making it longer. On Saturday, we ran out of time to do anything else, because Beryl was in Time Out for nearly three hours"

Herbertina Bunyon
Piddle in the Marsh.

Dr Esmeralda replies:

Dear Herbertina,

You poor thing, you really are trying very hard. But don't give up just yet. With just a few little tweaks, you will have Time Out working a treat. First, we shouldn't always believe the little monkeys when they say they enjoy Time Out. They do tell fibs sometimes – so as not to give us the satisfaction of winning! That said, do have a little think about the area that you use for Time Out – is there any reason why she might really be enjoying it – is there something nice to play with, or a book or a television perhaps? If so, time to think of somewhere else.

When you have chosen the right Time Out area, just ignore Beryl when she says she enjoys it. Once her 5 minutes is up, and she has been quiet for two minutes, let her out. I think you will find it starts working pretty soon. There is no need to keep going for 3 hours – that will probably just make her angry and irritable – not what a busy Mum wants!

What is time out?

Time out is like 'SUPER IGNORE'

Time out is a great way of showing your children what they must not do. *Smacking* is also used by parents but there are problems:

- Everyone gets upset
- Children become anxious
- Children learn that it is OK to hit
- You can't use it when they get bigger than you!

Behaviours that you can use TIME OUT for:

- Dangerous behaviours, e.g. rough fighting
- Destructive behaviours, e.g. breaking things
- Harmful behaviours, e.g. throwing things

How to use time out?

✓ Always choose a boring area for time out. For example, sitting in a corridor or a hallway. Bedrooms are not a good idea because they are usually full of toys and should be associated with nice times.

✓ Give a clear instruction and warning before using time out. For example, 'Put your foot down and stop kicking the door, or you will have to go to time out'.

✓ If they won't go to time out, respond immediately. Take them by the arm, firmly but calmly, or pick them up and explain that you are taking them to time out because what they did was wrong or dangerous and not allowed.

✓ Don't give attention during time out. Don't look at them, talk to them, or touch them, unless you really have to.

✓ Sometimes children leave time out before their time is up. Stay calm and return the child.

✓ Tell them when their time is up. If they say they don't want to come out, just leave them there.

✓ After they finish time out, look for the next good thing that they do, and give them lots of praise for it.

2

Consequences

Tips for using Consequences

- Consequences can be used for times when your child is non-compliant, or for dangerous behaviours if you feel you are using time out too much.
- Give one warning, and then if you don't get the behaviour that you want, give the child the consequence.
- Give the consequence as soon as you possibly can.
- Make the consequence mild and appropriate and make sure it is not something that is scary, or removing a basic right.
- Once you've given a consequence, stick to it.
- Once the consequence is over, forget about it, and give your child praise for some good behaviour as soon as ever you can.

Examples of good consequences

- ✓ The TV gets turned off for half an hour
- ✓ There will be no more playstation for the rest of the day
- ✓ You can't watch the match on TV this afternoon
- ✓ We will have to leave the park and go home now
- ✓ You will have to do some extra chores around the house (but make sure that this is something that you know you can make them do).
- ✓ You will have no sweets on the way home from school today

Write a list of consequences that you think will work for your child:

_____
_____
_____
_____
_____
_____
_____
_____
_____
_____
_____
_____
_____

Session Ten

Wrapping Up: Review, Managing School, Celebration

▶ Overview

In this session, after feedback from the previous session, we wrap up the course. We give parents an opportunity to ask any final questions, and spend some time talking about using new-found skills to help schools do their best for an anxious child. Finally, we give out certificates and celebrate the achievements that have been made over the past 10 sessions.

▶ Before the Session

- Arrange room as described in Chapter Two.
- Laminate 'principles' from Session Nine and stick them, and principles from previous sessions on the wall.
- Stick 'ground rules' from Session One on the wall.
- Stick up a large 'Seven Confident Thoughts' poster in a prominent location.
- Stick up the 'Anxiety Pyramid' poster.
- Print and laminate certificates for group members.

▶ The Session – Part 1

- **Welcome families**
- **Feedback on home practice**

Feedback should follow the general guidance on feedback on home practice that is given in Chapter Two.

Content of feedback

Feedback should be focused mostly on issues raised in Sessions Four and Nine, that is, Stairway to Bravery and time out and consequences. However, it is also important to keep referring back to praise and rewards, Special Play, managing worry, Thoughts, Feelings and Behaviour (TFB) and The Attention Rule.

From Timid to Tiger: A Treatment Manual for Parenting the Anxious Child. By Dr Sam Cartwright-Hatton with Dr Ben Laskey, Dr Stewart Rust and Dr Deborah McNally
© 2010 John Wiley & Sons, Ltd.

Stairway to Bravery

See Chapter Seven for guidance on feedback on Stairway to Bravery.

Special Play

See Chapter Five for guidance on feedback on Special Play.

TFB, The Seven Confident Thoughts and The Attention Rule

Remember to also refer back to TFB, Seven Confident Thoughts and The Attention Rule as much as possible.

Managing worry

See Chapter Eleven for guidance on feedback on managing worry.

Time out and consequences

Questions to ask:

- Who has had a chance to try the time out technique that we talked about in the last session?
- What situation did you use it in?
- What did you say?
- What did you do?
- Where did you do it (a safe, boring place)?
- How long did you do it for (one minute for each year of the child's age, up to a maximum of five, and until the child had been calm for two minutes)?
- Did you manage to not speak to your child and not touch your child (except to return them to time out, if they left)?
- How did your child respond?
- Did you manage to praise your child soon afterwards?
- What did you do next?
- How did that make you feel?
- How do you think your child felt?
- How did this help the Seven Confident Thoughts?
- Did anyone try using consequences?
- Did you manage to stick to the consequence?
- What consequence did you use? Did it fit the crime and was it something meaningful to the child?
- How soon did you give the consequence (as soon as possible)?
- Did the child have a chance to learn to get his/her behaviour right soon after the consequence?
- Once it was over, was the consequence forgotten about?

Troubleshooting feedback

Some of the feedback time should be spent discussing the time out and consequence techniques that were taught in Session Nine. This can raise a number of issues for parents that can stop them from using the techniques properly. Suggestions for dealing with these are reprinted from Chapter Eleven.

- I am scared to punish my child – he/she gets so upset.
  Many of the families that we see have been trained by their children so as not to impose any limits on their behaviour. They very often have children who become distressed easily, and are then difficult to console. So, for the sake of a quiet family life, and to protect their children from distress, the parents have stopped setting limits. However, if this is the case for any of your families, you should get them to consider the effects that this will have on the Seven Confident Thoughts. In general, families that have a clear set of rules and a clear, reliable set of consequences for breaking them have more confident children, who know that the world is a safe place, and who feel in control of what happens to them. Without these boundaries, children never know what is round the corner. We find that although a lot of the parents whom we see are quite lax in their rule enforcement, this makes family life very stressful, and these parents are *more* prone to snapping and imposing harsh and unfair punishments that really do cause their children genuine upset. In summary, a few rules, fairly and consistently applied are *good* for anxious children, and parents should not feel afraid to use them. In the case of very anxious parents, they may need to be encouraged to take very small steps towards using consequences and time out for the first time.

▶ The Session – Part 2

What to expect now

It is important that parents recognise that all of us have good days and bad days, and that we will all have times when things seem to get on top of us. Children are no different. There is a risk that when children go through a bad patch, parents panic and think that they are going 'back to square one'. When this happens, parents often forget all of the new techniques that they have learnt, and slip back to old, over-learnt strategies, running the risk of reinforcing the child's resurgence of anxiety symptoms. So, we discuss how things will be from now onwards. We ask parents if they can expect things to just get better and better, or if they should expect that sometimes it will feel like 'two steps forwards and one step back'? Most parents, when this is made explicit, recognise that they should not expect entirely smooth progress. We discuss the difference between a 'lapse' which is just a temporary setback and a 'relapse' which is more serious, and encourage parents to view difficulties as lapses rather than relapses.

Second, parents are encouraged to acknowledge how much they have learnt. They are asked to spend a moment reflecting on the improvements that their children have made. These improvements are down to the hard work of the parents in the group, and they should be encouraged to give themselves a pat on the back for this. At the same time, many parents of anxious children are perfectionists themselves. They should also be encouraged to accept flaws in their own parenting. Every parent makes mistakes. The group leaders, if they are parents themselves, can share examples of times when they have 'got it wrong' (nothing too catastrophic . . .). An important message from this session is for parents to feel very proud of themselves and to be gentle with themselves when they make mistakes.

First aid kit

If parents are to expect lapses in their child's progress, then we need to arm them with strategies to manage these. So, we ask them to keep a 'first aid kit'. This contains a number of items:

- Anxiety Pyramid and handouts.
  In our clinic, we are usually happy for parents to have our contact details, and call us for some advice if they run into difficulties in the future. However, we prepare them, in

advance, for the first thing that we will ask them when they call. This is 'Have you been doing the Anxiety Pyramid?' This means, have you been doing Special Play for 10 minutes a day? Have you been praising and rewarding good behaviours? Have you been ignoring unwanted behaviours? Have you been using good consequences and time out? Have you been gently encouraging your child to drop avoidance? So, before parents call us, they should go back to their handouts, and make sure that they are doing all of these things.

- Personal list of 'what worked'.
  This course covers a lot of material, and all of it is important to a greater or lesser extent, for all parents. However, all parents find that there are some techniques that really hit the spot for their child. So, at this point, we give parents their personal handout for this week and ask them to fill in the section marked 'things that have been most useful with my child'.

- Peer support.
  We invite parents to swap telephone numbers and to keep in informal contact. Many of them have already done this by this stage, and use each other as a valuable resource for support, encouragement and revision of techniques.

Getting school to help

In this programme, we do not do any direct work with school, although if resources are available in your clinic, this can be a valuable extra component. Instead of taking responsibility for managing difficulties at school ourselves, we encourage parents, who now have a great deal of knowledge and skill in dealing with children's anxiety, to help school to manage any difficulties that arise there. We don't go into a lot of detail here, but we give parents a handout on getting school to help, and another handout that they can give directly to the school. These can be copied from the end of this chapter.

- *Talk to school.*
  The first step is to talk to school about difficulties that are happening there. Very often an anxious child will be avoiding certain school activities, such as assembly or physical education, and this needs to be tackled. Often there is little that the parents can do themselves once the child is in school, but with their new-found understanding of what causes and maintains anxiety, they can help school to manage things. We suggest that parents approach the class teacher first. If that is insufficient, we suggest that they track down the school Special Educational Needs Coordinator (SENCO). Other useful people to talk to are the school nurse or the head teacher.

- *Ask school to praise and reward brave behaviours.*
  The first thing that any school can do (and, frankly should already be doing . . .) is to be giving copious praise and reward for behaviours that children find difficult. So, if a child is anxious about certain activities, parents should ask school to encourage their child to take some small brave steps and then give lots of praise and reinforcement for these. Some schools are very amenable to this, and just need pointing in the right direction, for example, 'please can you give a bit of extra praise when Sarah joins in at playtime', 'please can you give Kyle a sticker when he puts his hand up in class' and so on. Some teachers, however, for unfathomable reasons, do not like to single out children for praise, or particularly, for small rewards such as stickers. If this is the case, parents might have to persuade the teacher to do this discretely for their child, and perhaps provide the stickers themselves. Alternative strategies include asking the teacher to note brave behaviours in the home – school communication book that most primary schools now have, so that the parents can do the praising and rewarding later. Not ideal, but better late than never.

- *Encouraging participation.*

  Schools can be fantastic places for anxious children. There are many, many opportunities for children to try new experiences in a safe, supported environment. So, parents should not be afraid of discussing their child's temperament with their teacher, and asking the teacher to gently push their child to try new things and expand their horizons. For example, the teacher could watch out for opportunities, such as new sports or music clubs, or positions of responsibility, such as prefect posts, and gently encourage the anxious child to try these out. And then follow this, of course, with copious praise and reinforcement.

- *Avoiding avoidance.*

  By now, parents are very well-versed in the evils of avoidance. They recognise that in avoiding activities, their children are allowing the dragon in their mountain to get bigger and stronger, and that the only way to conquer it is to go up that mountain and test out their fears. So, if children are being allowed to avoid activities at school, then they should devise a plan, in conjunction with school, to reduce this avoidance. This can be done in a graded way, using the fear hierarchy technique that parents will have been using for several weeks at home.

- *Ensure that avoidance is boring.*

  We have seen countless examples of well-meaning schools reinforcing avoidance by being a bit too nice. For example, one child who was very upset by assembly was allowed not to go. Instead, he was to sit in the receptionist's office, where, upon close investigation, he was being fed large quantities of chocolate biscuits and having nice cosy chats with the kindly secretary. Ask parents in your group why this might have been a problem ...? When we intervened, the child was allowed to continue avoiding assembly for a short time whilst a graded hierarchy was being put into place, but he had to spend assembly time doing nothing (and getting very bored) instead. Assembly soon became the more appealing option and his fear diminished dramatically. Parents are now in an excellent position to identify reinforcers that are working on their children, and to modify them as appropriate.

- *Help school to help your child.*

  Even if parents do not have the confidence to go in to school and start giving school advice on how their child's anxiety can be managed, they can at least take a few steps to make sure that they are not undermining school's efforts.

- *Keep drop-offs calm and tear-free.*

  By this stage, most parents are becoming aware of the effect that their behaviour has on their children. However, we find that school drop-off time is a particular flashpoint for emotion, and is a time when many parents find it difficult to remember to behave! So, we talk about the need to keep drop-off time calm and tear-free, even if their child is very upset. We ask parents what their child is learning if the parent looks upset at having to leave them at school. It sends a strong message that school really is an upsetting, frightening place, and that the parent is not confident that the child will be happy and safe there. It also sends a message that the parent is unhappy, and for some children, this will cause them to worry about the parent as well as about school. Parents might need to practice 'Botox Face' and the 'Oscar-Winning Performance' in this situation.

- *Don't criticise school in front of your child.*

  Sometimes, schools really can be very unhelpful and can even exacerbate a child's anxiety problems. Parents need to vent their annoyance about this, but their child is not the person to do this to. Ask parents what their child will learn if they are critical of school in front of them? We tell parents that once a child's trust in school is undermined by his/her parents, it is very difficult to win this trust back. So, if parents need to let off steam about an issue at school, they should be encouraged to do this, but well out of earshot of their child.

Certificates and party

At this point, all that remains is to celebrate the achievements of the group, and to say goodbyes. We give out achievement certificates, which we get signed and laminated, by calling up each parent individually to collect his/hers. At the same time, we summarise that parent's achievements; for example, if a parent has been particularly good at devising clever rewards for her child, she will be hailed as 'praise and reward queen'. We also hand parents the 'principles' that they have each devised. This gives a final opportunity for revision of important concepts from the course.

Finally, we have some nice cakes and spend the last moments of the group chatting, exchanging contact details and congratulating each other. We think it is important that parents leave the group feeling that they have achieved a lot, and that they are in a great position to help their child to go on to become the confident adult that they hope for.

Key messages for the session

- Be very proud of what you have done for your child, but *don't* expect yourself to be a perfect parent.
- Don't panic about setbacks. Go back to the pyramid and make sure you are using all of the techniques.
- Talk to school and share your knowledge with them.

▶ Parental Cognition to be Elicited and Challenged

- I can't do this on my own
  Many parents tell us that they are anxious about leaving the group. Even parents who have done admirably, and have clearly learnt what they need to know often say that they are afraid that it will all fall apart when they do not have the weekly group sessions to support them. We remind parents of their achievements, and ask them to think of times when they managed a difficult situation well on their own. Other group members are often very good at reminding such parents of times they have coped very well and of their achievements.

  We give parents reassurance that if they want a quick chat with us at any point in the future, they are welcome to phone up (as long as they have revisited their 'first aid kit' first). We have never found ourselves overburdened by this.

▶ Don't Forget . . .

- Although this is a manualised intervention, remember the unique individuals in your group. Try to think about how they will each respond to the material in this session.
- Keep drawing out 'principles' and referring back to those generated by group members in previous sessions.
- Keep giving out those stickers to model reward and so that parents have a ready supply to use at home.
- Have fun! If you have fun, so will the group members.

Condensed session plan/treatment checklist

Item/concept	Group leader	Tick when completed
Part 1		
Feedback on home practice *Focus on*: Time out and consequences Stairway to Bravery *Also touch on*: Special Play Praise, rewards and star charts TFB and The Attention Rule Managing worry		
Part 2		
What to expect now		
First aid kit Anxiety Pyramid Personal list of what worked Peer support		
Getting school to help Talk to school Praise and reward Encouraging participation Avoiding avoidance Ensure that avoidance is boring Help school to help your child		
Certificates and party		
Key messages to be covered		
Be very proud of what you have done for your child, but *don't* expect yourself to be a perfect parent		
Don't panic about setbacks. Go back to the pyramid and make sure you are using all of the techniques		
Talk to school and share your knowledge with them		
Key cognitions to be elicited and challenged		
I can't do this on my own		

Wrapping Up

This week, Dr Esmeralda answers your questions on life after the group.

"Dear Dr Esmeralda,

My Godfrey did so well while we were going to the group. His behaviour was much better, and he was getting braver and braver. But this last week has just been a disaster. He has been fighting with his brother and crying all the way to school. I'm so worried Dr Esmeralda, I think we are going back to square one!"

Gertrude Gristleworth

Great Bigwart

Dr Esmeralda replies:

Dear Gertrude,

You tried very hard during the group, and your efforts paid off. You showed that you can make a really big difference to little Godfrey's life. The thing is, children have their ups and downs – just like us. I'll bet you that Godfrey is just having a little phase. Perhaps something is going on that is making him a bit stressed at the moment. You have two choices Gertie, you can give up on all of your hard work, or you can go back to your pyramid, and try even harder. If you dig your heels in, and keep trying hard, rest assured, Godfrey will soon start doing well again. I know you can do it Gertie, and remember….. TFB!"

"Dear Dr Esmeralda,

I am really rather worried about some of the advice you have been giving out. You seem to be happy with very low standards. You told one lady that she should just accept that her child will be naughty sometimes. I don't think this is right. Surely children should learn to behave all of the time?"

Will Missyou-Hall

Manchester

Dr Esmeralda replies:

Dear Will,

I do understand your concern. We all want our children to be a credit to us. It feels very difficult when they are disobedient or rude, or won't do something because they are scared. But you know Will, all of these things, in small doses, are completely normal. It is a rare child who is always good. It is an even rarer child who is never scared. The best parents are the ones who understand this. The best parents know that their children don't do things just to wind them up. Usually they are doing things for attention, or for reassurance – quite normal and healthy things for a little person to want. We should not ask our children to strive for perfection – they cannot achieve this any more than we can. Loosen up Will, and try to enjoy the good times with your kids!"

1

First aid kit

Some facts that you should know:

☺ Things *will* go wrong – your kids *will* have days when they are vile, and sometimes even whole weeks.

☺ No kid is perfect. Your kid *will* get things wrong, *will* still drive you mad, *will* still have fears and worries. All of this is completely normal.

☺ There is no such thing as the perfect child.

☺ There is no such thing as the perfect parent.

- -

So, what do you do when things go wrong?

☺ Tell yourself it is just a lapse, and never give up!

☺ Get out your handouts and do some revision.

☺ Look at the pyramid.

☺ Look at the things that have particularly helped you.

- -

Things that have been most useful with my child:

....
....
....
....
....
....
....
....
....

Advice for Parents

The first thing to do is to talk to your child's school. Just knowing that your child is having some emotional problems may well trigger some helpful responses from school. Most teachers have little or no training in how to deal with anxiety and depression, so they may well feel out of their depth. Do not feel embarrassed about sharing your knowledge of your child and of child anxiety, and making suggestions that have helped you at home.

How to get school on your side

Talking to teachers can feel a bit intimidating. However, things have moved on since we were at school, and most teachers now welcome involvement from parents, and are expected to treat family members' queries and comments with respect. So, even if you feel a bit anxious about doing it, do go and have a chat with school.

Teachers, however, are incredibly busy people, and many of them are very stressed. It can be very difficult for them to make special arrangements for just one child. Do bear this in mind when you are asking for special help for your child. Just acknowledging that you know how busy they are, and that you

would like to negotiate what it is possible for them to do within the limited resources that they have available, will help get you on their right side.

Who do I talk to?

The best person to approach to start with is probably your child's class teacher. Other good people to talk to are the School Nurse, or the school Special Educational Needs Coordinator (SENCO).

What do I tell them?

Just be open and honest and tell them all of the concerns that you have. If you have some concerns about how school are managing the problem, don't feel afraid to say this. However, try hard not come across as aggressive or complaining.

When going to schools, it is really useful to plan what you want to say in advance, and try to have a clear idea of what you want to achieve in the meeting. This way, you can get through the meeting quickly (always viewed positively by teachers) and come out with some concrete decisions made.

Working with any large organisation, such as a school, can sometimes be frustrating. Most schools have very few staff to deal with very many children, and teachers are often over-worked. Sometimes it feels as if things don't happen as quickly or as easily as they should. In these circumstances, it is very easy to get annoyed, and tempting to make a stroppy phone call to the Head Teacher. Although this feels like a good vent for emotions at the time, it almost always has very negative consequences in the long run. In our experience, the parents who get the best out of schools are the ones who are persistent and determined, but who also do all of their talking with a smile on their face. Teachers are like anyone else, they will bend to a bit of pressure, but are much more likely to do this for someone they like and feel warm towards. So, even if you get really annoyed with school, put down that telephone! Wait until you are a bit calmer before you call.

Practical steps that school can take

Positive discipline: The most useful thing that a school can do is make sure that it is a positive, happy place for children to be. Schools can do a lot to foster the Seven Confident Thoughts in children. However, to do this, they need to be places that are relatively calm, predictable, and fair. Most schools now attempt to achieve this, and do so by using positive discipline - the same as we do in the group. As we know from the anxiety pyramid, schools need to focus on rewarding positive behaviour before they attempt to reduce negative behaviour using consequences. If your school don't seem to know what the rules for good behaviour management are, tell them what we've talked about on the course, and show them your handouts. Basically, the rules for managing behaviour in schools are:

* School staff should watch out for good behaviour and give good clear praise when they see it.
* School staff should decide on a type of good behaviour that they really want to encourage (e.g. trying hard at schoolwork, acts of kindness, etc) and reward these using stickers or other small prizes.
* The rules about behaviour should be clear to all - parents, teachers, support staff, and, of course, the children. Everyone should know what behaviour is not allowed, and of course, what behaviour will get praise and reward.
* Everyone should know what will happen if bad behaviour is seen
* Consequences for unwanted behaviour should be: Not severe

   Understood by everyone

   Consistently applied

   Given out as soon as possible
* Once a consequence is out of the way, the unwanted behaviour should be forgotten about.

Encouraging children to take part

Anxious children really benefit from taking part in lots of social activities, even if they don't feel like it. School is a great source of opportunities for this. Teachers and other school staff such as playground supervisors and lunchtime supervisors can be real allies for the parent who wants to get their kid engaging in more social activities.

Explain to school why social activities are so good for your child and ask them to lend a hand in getting your child active at school. They can do this by keeping an eye out for your child.

If they spot your child standing in a corner doing nothing, ask them to suggest some activities to your child, and, especially for younger children, pair them up with a friendly and helpful child who can chivvy them into activities.

Being firm but kind about avoidance

There are many school-based activities that anxious children find very hard. Based on the children that we have seen, we would say that the following activities are the most likely to cause them problems:

* Assemblies
* Lunchtime
* Physical Education / games
* Lessons that they struggle with academically
* Tasks that require public speaking for example, reading out aloud, school plays.

We now know that avoiding scary activities causes big problems in the long run (remember the Dragon in the Mountain...?), and children should be encouraged to face up to the activities if they can. If your child has developed a real phobia of these activities, just forcing him/her to take part may not be the right way to go. In this situation, use the Stairway to Bravery.

However, if your child hasn't got a phobia of the situation, and just finds it very unpleasant, it is best to encourage him/her to take part as much as he/she can. Of course, when your child is trying to avoid something at home, you will be on hand to encourage him/her to face his/her fear, but at school, you will not be. In this case, you will be relying on the teachers to do the job for you. If you know that your child tries to avoid a particular part of school life, ask the teacher:

* To watch for your child trying to avoid the activity. Many kids will do this by complaining that they don't feel very well or by acting out.

* If your child tries to avoid the activity, firmly but calmly and kindly tell them that they need to take part, even if they don't feel like it.

* Once your child has taken part in the activity, give them praise for coping well. A little reward might also help. (It might help to leave a little bag of rewards at school, so that the teacher has some to hand). If school are not happy with providing rewards for just one child, get them to give your child a sticker, which he / she can trade in for a little reward from you, later in the day.

* If your child refuses to take part in the activity because of fear, they should *never* be punished. However, they should always be given an alternative activity to do. This alternative activity is to make sure that they don't get to use the spare time to do something nice, which

would act as a reward for their avoidance. Ask the teacher to find an activity for your child to do while they are avoiding. This activity should be as boring as humanly possible. Since you will know your child better than the teacher, you could suggest something that you know your child will find intensely boring. For instance, one child might find placing piles of exercise books in alphabetical order intensely boring, whilst another might find it quite pleasing. Talk with the teacher to make sure that time spent avoiding an activity does not end up being fun! Depending on the child, they may need to be supervised whilst doing this, but try to make sure that this supervision does not end up being a nice cosy chat with the friendly school secretary! Remember, any time spent avoiding an activity should be made to be really, really boring.

Clear and reasonable expectations for pupils' academic performance

Schools can be fantastic for raising your anxious child's self esteem. There is so much scope in school for mastering new skills, and achieving targets. However, whether these are translated into boosts to your child's self esteem depends, to some extent, on how this is managed by your child's school.

Clear goals

The best schools have clear goals for children. The kids know what they are meant to achieve, and they know who they will tell when they have got there. When they do achieve, the kids get loads of praise for this. Check whether this is happening in your child's school. Does your child know what each teacher expects of him / her?

Manageable goals

It might be a good idea to check that the levels expected of your child are reasonable. Expectations should be tailored to each child, and if your child is very anxious, these expectations should be reduced for the time being – lots of research shows that it is difficult to do well at schoolwork when you are struggling with severe anxiety. If your child's school are not aware of this, please do tell them to be prepared for poorer academic performance from your child until the problems are sorted out.

Communicating success to pupils

Even when high academic standards are met, not all schools are good at communicating this success to children. This a particular problem for anxious kids, as they can be prone to comparing themselves too much to other children.

How can you help school to help you?

Keep them posted

Do talk to school. They can only help your child if they know that there is a problem, and if they know what to do.

•Keep drop-offs calm and tear free

Bringing up an anxious child is a big strain on a parent's emotions. When your child is crying or distressed, it is easy to become upset yourself. School drop-off time is a real flashpoint for these emotions. However, if you can cover up  your own distress, then your child will cope much better. If your child starts crying, try not to join in! Instead, give them a big smile, tell them to have a lovely day, and shove them through the door, before retiring to the car with a big box of tissues.

Avoid complaining about school in front of your child

Sometimes schools do things that don't help, and if so, you need to vent your frustration about this. However, we would strongly urge you to do this when your child is well out of earshot. As we have discussed on the course, children copy their parents, and easily take on their parents' opinions. If your child knows that you don't have confidence in the school, then they will lose confidence too. This is a slippery slope to go down. Once the child loses confidence in their school, it becomes very difficult for the parents to convince them that it is a safe and happy place for them to go.

Advice for Teachers

Anxiety

Anxiety is the most common psychological problem of childhood. Conservative estimates suggest that about 4% of children are struggling with an anxiety disorder at any one time. Anxiety disorders in pre-adolescent children can manifest in a number of ways, but most commonly as excessive fears and phobias, excessive worry, and difficulties separating from parents. Aggressive behaviour can also appear if these children are forced into doing things that are frightening for them.

Some children will grow out of their anxiety disorder, but many will not. For those who do not, a lifetime of anxiety, depression, difficulty with relationships and academic and occupational functioning can await. Fortunately, there is now much that can be done for these children.

How can I help?

You have been given this handout because a child in your class has been diagnosed with an anxiety disorder. The child's parent(s) have attended a course on managing their child's anxiety. However, there is also much that a school can do to help an anxious child grow in confidence. This leaflet outlines some of the key areas where schools and teachers can help. The child's parents will also be very familiar with the principles described in the leaflet, and will be happy to talk to you about what they have learnt on the course.

Practical steps that school can take

Positive discipline: The most useful thing that a school can do is make sure that it is a positive, happy place for children to be. To do this, schools need to be places that are relatively calm, predictable, and fair. Schools can achieve this by focussing on positive discipline. That is, by focussing on encouraging good behaviour using praise and reward, using clear, mild consequences, and avoiding criticism.

7

Positive Discipline

If discipline is to be used (and in reality, it is going to be needed sometimes in all schools) then it should follow the golden rules. Basically, the golden rules are:

* School staff watch out for good behaviour and give good clear praise when they see it.

* School staff decide on a type of good behaviour that they really want to encourage (e.g. trying hard at school-work, acts of kindness, etc) and reward these using stickers or other small prizes.

* The rules about behaviour should be clear to all – parents, teachers, support staff, and, of course, the children. Everyone should know what behaviour is not allowed and what behaviour is to be encouraged.

* Everyone knows what will happen if bad (and good) behaviour is seen

* Consequences for unwanted behaviour should be:

    Not severe   Given out as soon as possible
    Understood by everyone   Short, and ensure the child gets an opportunity
    Consistently applied   to 'get it right' ASAP.

* Once a consequence is out of the way, the unwanted behaviour should be forgotten about.

Encouraging children to take part

Anxious children really benefit from taking part in lots of social activities, even if they don't feel like it. School is a great source of opportunities for this. Teachers and other school staff such as playground supervisors and lunchtime supervisors can be real allies for the parent who wants to get their kid engaging in more social activities.

You can do this by keeping an eye out for the anxious child. If you spot this child standing in a corner doing nothing, suggest some activities to the child, and, especially for younger children, pair them up with a friendly and helpful child who can chivvy them into activities.

Being firm but kind about avoidance

There are many school-based activities that anxious children find very hard. Based on the children that we have seen, we would say that the following activities are the most likely to cause them problems:

* Assemblies
* Lunchtime
* P.E. / games
* Lessons that they struggle with academically.
* Tasks that require public speaking e.g. reading out aloud, school plays.

We now know that avoiding scary activities causes big problems in the long run, and children should be encouraged to face up to the activities if they can. However, if the child has developed a real phobia of these activities, just forcing them to take part may not be the right way to go. Parents on our course have learnt skills for dealing with these more severe fears, and will be able to work with you to draw up a plan for dealing with this in school (ask them to show you the handout on 'stairway to bravery'). However, if the child hasn't got a phobia of the situation, but just finds it very unpleasant, it is best to encourage them to take part as much as they can.

* Watch for the child trying to avoid the activity. Many kids will do this by complaining that they don't feel very well or by acting out.

* If the child tries to avoid the activity, firmly but calmly and kindly tell them that they need to take part, even if they don't feel like it.

* Once the child has taken part in the activity, give the child praise for coping well. A little reward might also help. The parents are familiar with the role of rewards, and should be happy to provide a selection of small rewards for you to use with their child. If you are not happy with providing rewards for just one child, give the child a sticker, which he / she can trade in for a little reward from the parent, later in the day.

9

* If the child refuses to take part in the activity because of fear, they should *never* be punished for this. However, they should always be given an alternative activity to do. This alternative activity is to make sure that they don't get to use this spare time to do something nice, which would act as a reward for their avoidance. If you give the child an activity to do while they are avoiding, this activity should be as boring as humanly possible. The child's parents may be able to suggest something that the child will find intensely boring.

E.g. One child might find placing piles of exercise books in alphabetical order intensely boring, whilst another might find it quite pleasing. Whatever you do, just make sure that time spent avoiding an activity does not end up being fun! Depending on the child, they may need to be supervised whilst doing this, but try to make sure that this supervision does not end up being a nice, cosy chat with the friendly school secretary! Remember, any time spent avoiding an activity should be really, really boring.

Clear and reasonable expectations for pupils' academic performance

Schools can be fantastic for raising an anxious child's self esteem. There is so much scope in school for mastering new skills, and achieving targets. However, whether these are translated into boosts to a child's self esteem depends, to some extent, on how this is managed by school:

* Clear goals

The best schools have clear goals for children. The children know what they are meant to achieve, and they know how they will tell when they have got there. When they do achieve, they get loads of praise for this.

* Manageable goals

It might be a good idea to check that the levels expected of the anxious child are reasonable. For a very anxious child, expectations should be reduced for the time being – lots of research shows that it is difficult to do as well as normal at schoolwork when you are struggling with severe anxiety.

* Communicating success to pupils

Even when high academic standards are met, not all schools are good at communicating this success to children. This is a particular problem for anxious kids, as they can be prone to comparing themselves too much to other children.

Additional Resources

► Professional Training Courses

For professionals seeking further training on working with parents, we recommend the following programmes. Although these are largely directed at helping families manage behaviour problems, the techniques that are taught are adaptable for use with anxious families, as outlined in this book.

- Webster-Stratton Parenting Training. A range of courses are available for practitioners who want to provide behavioural training programmes to parents. These range from 3-day courses to certification and are available in the United Kingdom and overseas. Further details are available at http://www.incredibleyears.com/
- Triple P training. A range of courses are available for practitioners who want to provide courses for parents at different levels, ranging from short courses to full certification. Courses are available worldwide. Further details are available at http://www.triplep.net/

For professionals seeking further training in CBT, we recommend the following resource.

- Training in cognitive behaviour therapy for anxiety (and other disorders) in adults and children is now available widely throughout the United Kingdom. For information on courses ranging from one-day workshops through to masters degree courses, see the list at www.babcp.com.

► Books for Professionals

- Carolyn Webster-Stratton, Martin Herbert (1994) *Troubled Families – Problem Children: Working with Parents – A Collaborative Process*, Wiley.
- Martin Herbert, Jenny Wookey (ed.) (2004) *Managing Children's Disruptive Behaviour: A Guide for Practitioners Working with Parents and Foster Parents*, Wiley Blackwell.
- Silverman, W.K., Field, A.P. (eds) (Due 2010) *Anxiety Disorders in Children and Adolescents: Research, Assessment and Intervention*, 2nd edn, Cambridge University Press.
- Peter Muris, Rachman, S.J. (ed.) (2007) *Normal and Abnormal Fear and Anxiety in Children and Adolescents* (BRAT Series in **Clinical Psychology**), Elsevier.
- Michael W. Vasey, Mark R. Dadds (eds) (2000) *The Developmental Psychopathology of Anxiety*, OUP.
- Paul Stallard (2005) *A Clinician's Guide to Think Good Feel Good: Using CBT with Children and Young People*, Wiley.

From Timid to Tiger: A Treatment Manual for Parenting the Anxious Child. By Dr Sam Cartwright-Hatton with Dr Ben Laskey, Dr Stewart Rust and Dr Deborah McNally
© 2010 John Wiley & Sons, Ltd.

▶ Books for Parents

- Carolyn Webster-Stratton (2006) *The Incredible Years*. This book is focused largely on behaviour problems, but provides a sympathetic and parent-friendly overview of many of the techniques that are taught in Timid to Tiger.
- Sam Cartwright-Hatton (2007) *Coping with an Anxious or Depressed Child*. Oneworld Publications.
- Cathy Creswell, Lucy Willetts (2007) *Overcoming your Child's Fears and Worries*. Constable & Robinson.
- Cathy Creswell, Lucy Willetts (2007) *Overcoming your Child's Shyness and Social Anxiety*. Constable & Robinson.
- Ron Rapee, Ann Wignall (2008) *Helping your Anxious Child: A Step by Step Guide for Parents*. New Harbinger Publications.

▶ Support for Parents

- General parenting support is now available in many areas of the United Kingdom. Most areas have a local 'Children's Information Service' (local number available in yellow pages or online) who collate information on what is available for parents in the area.
- Direct support for parents of children experiencing difficulties with anxiety is harder to come by than support for parents of children with other disorders. However, Anxiety UK, which is the United Kingdom's largest charity for sufferers of anxiety disorders, now has excellent resources for young sufferers of anxiety and their families. Detailed information on anxiety in childhood is available on their website at www.anxietyuk.org.uk/youngpeople.php. Other resources including peer support and CBT for anxiety (for children and adults) is available at low cost.

Index

Printed in Great Britain
by Amazon